SELECTED POEMS

Jaan Kaplinski is one of Estonia's best-known writers and cultural figures. He was born in Tartu in 1941, shortly after the Soviet annexation of Estonia. His mother was Estonian, and his Polish father died in a labour camp in northern Russia when Jaan was still a child. 'My childhood,' he has said, 'passed in Tartu, a war-devastated university town. It was a time of repression, fear and poverty.'

Jaan Kaplinski studied Romance Language and Linguistics at Tartu University and has worked as a researcher in linguistics, as a sociologist, ecologist and translator. He has lectured on the History of Western Civilisation at Tartu University and has been a student of Mahayana Buddhism and philosophies of the Far East. He has published several books of poetry and essays in Estonian, Finnish and English, and his work has been translated into many languages.

After publishing translations of three collections with Harvill in Britain, one of these from Breitenbush and one from Copper Canyon in the US, Kaplinski published *Evening Brings Everything Back* with Bloodaxe Books in 2004, a book combining work from three earlier titles published in Estonia, *Evening brings everything back* (1984), *Ice and Heather* (1989) and *Summers and Springs* (1995). His semi-autobiographical novel, *The Same River*, translated by Susan Wilson, was published by Peter Owen in 2009.

His *Selected Poems* (Bloodaxe Books, 2011) includes work previously unpublished in English as well as poems drawn from all four of his previous UK collections: *The Same Sea in Us All* (1985/1990), *The Wandering Border* (1987/1992), *Through the Forest* (1991/1996) and *Evening Brings Everything Back* (2004).

He has translated poetry from French, English, Spanish, Chinese and Swedish (a book of poems by Tomas Tranströmer), and travelled in many countries, including Britain, China, Turkey and parts of Russia. Awarded many prizes and honours, he is a member of several learned societies including the Universal Academy of Cultures. Jaan Kaplinski was a member of the new post-Revolution Estonian parliament (Riigikogu) in 1992-95 and his essays on cultural transition and the challenges of globalisation are published across the Baltic region. Further details and texts are on his website http://jaan.kaplinski.com

JAAN KAPLINSKI

SELECTED POEMS

TRANSLATED BY
JAAN KAPLINSKI
WITH
SAM HAMILL
HILDI HAWKINS
FIONA SAMPSON

BLOODAXE BOOKS

ISBN: 978 1 85224 889 5

First published 2011 by
Bloodaxe Books Ltd,
Highgreen,
Tarset,
Northumberland NE48 1RP.

www.bloodaxebooks.com
For further information about Bloodaxe titles
please visit our website or write to
the above address for a catalogue.

Supported by
**ARTS COUNCIL
ENGLAND**

Cover design: Neil Astley & Pamela Robertson-Pearce.

Printed in Great Britain by
Bell & Bain Limited, Glasgow, Scotland.

ACKNOWLEDGEMENTS

This selection includes poems previously unpublished in English as well as work drawn from all four of Jaan Kaplinski's previous collections of poems translated into English: *The Same Sea in Us All* (Breitenbush Books, USA, 1985; Collins Harvill, UK, 1990), *The Wandering Border* (Copper Canyon Press, USA, 1987; Harvill, UK, 1992), *Through the Forest* (The Harvill Press, UK, 1996), and *Evening Brings Everything Back* (Bloodaxe Books, 2004), which drew on three books, *Evening brings everything back* (1984), *Ice and Heather* (1989) and *Summers and Springs* (1995).

Through the Forest was published in Estonian as *Tükk elatud elu* by Eesti Kostabi Selts (Tartu) in 1991; *Evening brings everything back* as *Õhtu toob tagasi kõik* by Eesti Raamat (Tallinn) in 1984; *Summers and Springs* as *Mitu suve ja kevadet* by Vagabund (Tallinn) in 1995.

The Soul Returning is previously unpublished in English translation. Three translations originally published in *The Wandering Border* ('No one can put me back together again', 'And when the sea retreats from here', 'Night comes and extinguishes the numbers') are republished here as part of *The Same Sea in Us All*, where they belong. Three of the twelve poems in the section *Poems Written in English* ('Karl Barth, Paul Tillich, Karl Rahmer', 'Coming home', 'Om svabhavasuddhah sarva dharmah') appeared in *The Wandering Border*; the other nine poems are previously unpublished.

Special thanks are due to Arts Council England for providing a translation grant for this book.

Jaan Kaplinski wishes to thank Sam Hamill, Hildi Hawkins and Fiona Sampson for their work on the translations from Estonian, and Lawrence Kitching for editorial help with poems written in English.

CONTENTS

FROM **THE WANDERING BORDER** (1987)

THE SOUL RETURNING (1973-75)

POEMS WRITTEN IN ENGLISH

from

THE SAME SEA IN US ALL

(1985)

translated by
JAAN KAPLINSKI
with SAM HAMILL

Sails come sailing out
from foreign pictures
sails on the Yangtze
sails on the River Li

Sun
golden fish swimming over green rocks
sky with birds
seen through falling petals

Look to the east the shadow
of a white cloud
slants over glittering water
on the horizon
emerging
white sails   sails   sails

*

Our shadows are very long
when we return at night from haying
but we ourselves are small

The camomile clasps its hands together
as if in prayer
A woman with a sickle creeps up the hill
as she did a thousand years ago

Beyond the courtyard
the heath
beyond the heath forest

Heather heather-coloured
whither dost thou fly little bee
that heaven
is so vast and void
once we will return
once we will all return.

*

Only to go along, only to go along,
always there is spring somewhere,
there is rain somewhere.

Only to go along, only to go hand in hand with spring
where there was a desert yesterday, where he who goes
was himself a desert yesterday, full of mirages and memories
where red and yellow poppies like armies
rise from the dead;
only to go and see with one's own eyes there's no need to stay,
no need to finish anything before going on, no need to guard the
    grave
on this morning of the resurrection of the yellow poppies.

Only to go along, no need to take a thing,
no need to return, no need to return from that
third morning of desert flowers
to oneself, to one's headache, angina pectoris, white bedsheets,
the place of one's grave:
only to see, only to be with him,
to be with poppies, cacti, amaryllises, mesembryanthemums.

Let him who believes in duty fold the sheets,
let someone advertise a free gravesite in the papers.
One who was sick, one who had been buried, was lost without a
    trace
on the third day.

Two days ago, the thunderbird broke its shell
and they all heard it: lilies, amaryllises, poppies, the hedgehog
    heads of cacti,
and the mesembryanthemums in their stony sleep.
Yesterday the grass burned on the savannah, the dry blades of grass.
and today they are all here, only you have to come to see –

only to come and look, catch him and follow him,
follow the spring that walks somewhere over the listening earth:
he is always somewhere, he is always everywhere.

*

You, you moon – in whose laps did you place darkness
  before there was night?
Do you remember, the day stood before the new pages
  and didn't dare come in.
March waited at the head of the bed blowing her fists,
  April emerged from the sea-foam.
Everything else was just the wind whistling,
  burnt books flying overhead.
Do you remember the resurrection, have you forgotten the life?
After all, you know where we were buried. Put
  your ear to the ground and listen:
a train faraway? No! No armour, no pneumatic hammer, no –
  air rustling in the pits of lungs, pulse beating.
The light brings back the white butterfly from beyond Pluto's orbit.

*

White clover asks nothing
but when they ask in whose name
I will reply in the name of white clover

only bones and tin buckles remain after soldiers
resin has eaten the crosses from the pines
white white white clover

one stalk three leaves: Father Son Holy Spirit
dark needles bark fluttering in the wind
crimson was the question green is the answer

    *

Who has who has ever
rowed across the river
to other shore
is always
across the river

here and there
the same yellow buttercups
are burning into ashes

*

O distant sun
faceless nameless
silvering light
flashing on fish
lake blooming its blooming
bird
calls to bird
from dusk to dawn
sleeping rustling rushes

————

word only words
empty vessels in empty space
everything else
is one and the same – a world
which never was
and never will be

nobody is and cannot
be anything – what
does this solitude mean

————

Blue – too blue
high swing above the shore
strange sun and wind

ants
scattered over bare sand
carnations rise from the earth
the land
belongs to us to me to no one

*

If you want to go
do not remain if only for our sake
because we do not understand – thirty years
forty years of thirst of sunsets and sunrises in dusty windows
who then can say to us whither and how long yet
who then will answer us if you
take your hand
from your mother's hand
from your father's hand
and the wind takes your hand and you go

    on aspen leaves
    the tiny feet of the sun walk
    into evening
    today always and for a long time yet

we are given too much and we are
very poor
we are taught too much and we know
nothing

    but we too we do not want
    to inhabit the same world
    as an Oliver Cromwell or a Josef Stalin

but we must remain – wagons
athwart, sideways on the road
we have no speech and no voice if you go
look back once more wait

    fields are fanning green scarves
    meadows are fanning motley scarves
    you are melting away between grass and bumblebees

the road rises and descends again
you go and will not return – the hands of a windmill
are waving when you are already on the other side of the hill
when we all are we all will be

everyday life hair grows even after death
free time motorcycles cathalepsy
paraplegy anabiosis crimes and punishments

we shall all be free we shall see
what it really is it will anyway have an end
and we have enough time do not go before us wait
some time some mile on the king's dismal plain
in the land of burnt tanks and turning wheels
because we must find the way

long sandy straight openings
to put your head on the naked knees of the forest
and sleep until the end

when you forget us and smile to the windmill on the hillside
and go away who will help us
to the gate and say to them there
that we are back

white rivers are lost in white sand
yellow rivers are lost in yellow sand
in the blue eyes of my child
the land beyond forests shines

home shelter courtyard well
rooster's crow opening buds
all awake with all all together with all

but nothing is ready yet
nothing will ever be ready
in the long dreams of the children
is God Himself dreaming of His dreams

the windmill is playing with wind the road rises and descends again
do not go yet remain
remain with us for we do not yet know a thing

a red cloud cuts the sun into halves
the sky is full of marlets

*

Every dying man
is a child:
in trenches, in bed, on a throne, at a loom,
we are tiny and helpless
when black velvet bows our eyes
and the letters slide from the pages.
Earth lets nobody loose: it all
has to be given back – breath, eyes, memory.
We are children when the earth
turns with us through the night towards morning
where there are no voices, no ears, no light, no door,
only darkness and movement
in the soil and its thousands
of mouths, chins, jaws, and limbs
dividing everything so that
no names and no thoughts remain
in the one who is silent lying in the dark
on his right side, head upon knees.
Beside him, his spear, his knife
and his bracelet, and a broken pot.

*

They are standing up to their knees in blood and mud,
up to their knees, *not on their knees*,
at the gas chambers, *not gas stoves*,
saying that life is beautiful...
I cannot, I cannot once more...

The world is a dark surface,
a polished surface aslant, aslant,
a world aslant towards Auschwitz,
aslant my town,
my town, my home, my wife and child
high up on the thin edge – below,
only smooth polished wood,
black wood, and high up
you, me, all of us
and looking down one feels
his heart falling, his blood flowing straight down,
down – *no one is strong enough*,
nobody demolished the gas chambers,
nobody made peace:
this all exists from the beginning,
war in peace, peace in war. All in all,
how long can we stand here, how long
believing life is beautiful,
that *everyone gets his due*, that *work makes us free*?
Under millions of eyes that are ashes
we are standing on a sleek thin board
above millions of eyes that are ashes.

Only together with them might one be happy,
and they are looking at me with millions of eyes
and my pale blood is flowing straight down
hoping to find a pure hope, a handful of pure land
under the sun's distorting mirror, under this slanting land,

these white clouds and the jubilant endless indifference
of the last skylarks.
My love, I am again falling on my eyes
into the ashes of those I could have been,
on my eyes into their burnt eyes
as if it were not painful enough to be born
on white sheets under a dark light
to become executioner or victim. I know
that everything is
only lightning reflected in dewdrops, suffering
the more distant, the more real, what was forgotten
returns in this way, towers breaking, railways melting,
fishes drowning – my eyes, why
do you not help me – dead,
why do you not help me to live – the Creator
has not yet said his first word? But
has the end not ended, the beginning not begun?
Everything is something else *for him*
who writes and reads, but no one of us
speaks truth when he says he knows why,
whither, with what, to whom, how long
we are said, written, shaped
to have a meaning. – Even that
is too much for words. PEACE
is too big. In peace
there is room for everything. But how
can I be there together with those that are not,
how can killers be together with the killed
meaning one and the same thing. TOO MUCH
you are to me, world, why
didn't you leave me in your unconscious
flowering clover?

*

28

Everything is inside out, everything is different –
colourless, nameless, voiceless –
the sky overhead is an axe-blade. No one knows
that what mirrors the stars and the Milky Way is an axe.
Only those who love see, and remain silent
while in the sky the mirror-blade gets loose and falls
through us, a black starry dark
falling through a blacker dark, and nothing can stop it.
It falls no matter how we turn, always,
it hits us and divides head from body.
The sound of the abyss rises like clouds through us.
Twin stars are overhead: one light, one dark.
Everything else is illimitable void and distant,
dust motes whirling through a dark cathedral, everything else
is a black shawl where the fine old fire has written our names too.

*

Sleep covers us too much for one, too little for two.
Your toes are naked in defiance of the winter night.
Red foxes move like flames in the mountains,
Pentatonics: your little finger *is* little,
and on your closed eyelids the middle and elder brothers
slide back into the fairytale.

But some day much later, I will recall the shore,
awakening beside you after death in a dream.
There are broken trees and splinters of ships
and crosses for the departed who, perhaps, have arrived.
Once, the sheet will glide from us. Once, the eyes will stiffen
and a common grave will hold the brothers. If then, too,
if then too, what then? Why? What, my love?

*

Non-being pervades everything and being is full of peace.
Your translation of Lao-tse can be right or wrong – an open book
speaks today as an open butterfly and in the pollen
movement meets immobility in the same way.
The spring breeze flows through our hair and clothes.
If I speak, it is because the consolation is so much more
than ourselves waiting for it: waters breaking in from everywhere,
the tent-roof taking flight in the clear night of Lappland,
necklaces falling shattered: phrases, life and wisdom.
So this is it, this is you. The eyes are melting
in the white clouds, it is love, love that cuts us
from squared paper and lets the fire warm us
and the rain come through us until between the earth and us
the last borderlines vanish. This is love: the leaves of trees
and the light like ourselves full of evidence of the infinite.
We shall be and we shall be what is not,
we shall remain what belongs to no one.

*

No one can put me back together again
fingering broken strings you thought perhaps of something else
all cells and scales are silent, ready to answer to questions
which see through, come through, us, objects, fields, rays
which are united by nothing other than truth, the empty word,
     the sea, the ocean
where we were constructed, put together bone by bone, cell by cell,
     syllable by syllable
is he who writes poetry nightly me
with aching back, with grey hair, with your name, with thought
     only of you
and you come and stand in my room in my eyes in me
and your hands are warm, salty, most beloved
hands which wipe the dust from old letters for the knowledge that
we have been, we have died, we have been born of the dark people
of whom there are so few words and so many graves' heavy stones
that he who rests would have peace on the ash and on the splinters
     of bone, what, what
were you thinking, girl opening the doors of the promontory with
     the keys of fairytales
and asking me for the palmar lines of the megaliths
what were you thinking, Love, fingering my broken fingers by
     candlelight

     *

32

And when the sea retreats from here before or after the splitting
   of the personality

we may still go to be there, to step in the sandpiper's tracks

remain in the wind, remain in the rain in the summer and winter
   in freedom

because another you and I do not exist and the horizon remains
   always behind the horizon

to share all the bread that remains, the joy, the snow which does
   not preserve or forbid

the sun's turning around the equinoctial dark apple trees in gardens

for you, for me, for me who half this life has twined rope and
   performed under someone's name

trusted flags and entropy plucked out dead nettles

dreaming of wings, wings,

who stands with eyes wide open in a coloured room which you tied

from my fingers with your fingers into one

   *

Night comes and extinguishes the numbers and the year
lifts us from the past and brings away
from the checkerboard table from among kings queens and knights
the wind's silence and the source the seventh witness
which is a tiny beginning, roots, our infinite roots
wakening still sleeping still in stone crevices in soil
without knowing oneself even without understanding who he is
    who is woven into them
through the dark earth thus the trees meet all at once in the upper
    and lower world through mother's mute flesh
fingers with fingers, leaves with leaves, loins with loins,
silently blood and earth fall from between us
your young body bursts into flames under dry leaves

*

Once more spring pulls young leaves from buds
and the earth hides its tears under primrose.
But a man is only a ship anchored in himself, in his history,
his time, a big ship decaying on the village pond
forgetting there are other beings, other societies and worlds:
fishes building nests or surfacing to breathe,
caravans of penguins arriving on the shore,
ants walking their ancient trails – the soil is alive and moves
its endless feet, flagella, mouth, appendages and antennae.
But a man should be clear, a mirror reflecting everything:
this spring, these birds returning, these triangles, open
and closed sets, and hierarchies –
a man is curved, a closed surface reflecting only himself,
the ancient darkness in his vaults
where even candlelights are weary and names written with soot
cover one another. Everyone wants to perpetuate himself,
one conquers, one discovers, one wins: all looking for
themselves, for their sooty names, suitable place
on the walls and under the vaults of history.
The darkness is deep. And cold carbonic acid gas is rising
and white eyeless fishes are stirring in their pools,
niches in sandstone, everywhere mummies and pyramids of bones,
too little space for the living.
Small indeed is the consolation from what once was said
by another buried alive, small consolation from churches
and castles, from painting and classical music.
A man finds himself moved far away from the living:
beside him, above him, beneath him.
He is closed in himself and has invented his own reflection
and the reflection of that reflection: culture, literature,
architecture. But even this is hopelessly, hopelessly little.
But then? But then, as from another space, from a world
from under other suns, the language of the bees, the intelligence

of dolphins, a little understanding, satori, some open space
in the catacombs of our minds. A little consolation
in the oxygen deficiency.
Some wind in the grey lobes in the sclerotic vessels see
something bursting like a spring in the *fossa sylvii*
hippocampus the little sea horse skipping in its paradise of algae
before the windows are locked with bars and the city escapes
into its soot and noise. My leaves are too white,
too futile to compare with the green, a petty testimony
compared to the sparrow's song, a testimony of the truth
that eyes are proof of seeing, ears are proof of hearing,
and no alphabet, no code, no axiom. Never. And nowhere.

*

Light
reminds us
of something
through
the roof of
the old barn
even
when the young
grass is
already grown
through the wings

ant-path
on the eyes
your ashes
our ashes
wandering
with the rains
of centuries:
irrevocably
bound

        *

Oven
alone
in the corner

grandmother
alone
in the graveyard

the same
big grey
handmill:

the wind
of May
rolls
over us

   *

What woke us
was indeed nothing
but a dancing pea
in a turning cathedral

a little turning
girl blowing
dandelion-paratroopers
into every wind

and walls looking
towards her through
walls and the voice
returns to the beginning

*

Night and earth
breathing in the warmth
of the past day

as yours is only
what will not
be left to you

a day a thought a life
handful of foam
trembling on the sand
in wind into wind

under the seventh lock
a bird's voice
is singing
of something else

but no key
to it
in any
human tongue

wind
lick clean
stones and
our eyes
with your warm
moist
salty tongue

*

To be
Icarus
and fall
wings aflame
into
the burning
buttercups
which

recapture
your own
nameless
fatherland

some passage
some island
some Utopia

gets
your name

*

Honeybees
through
sunshine

rising
dancing
falling
dust:

a moment of
being
so full
of joy

even
without
any wish
that everyone
read
from your glance
the end
of the poem

*

You
light-footed moss
already
on
the window frame
already
on the roof

to walk
on tiny
feet
which
arrived
so long
before you

on fingers
which
guarded you
in the almost
intolerable
world

long
before
you knew
how
to see
them
and
name them

*

Near
nearest
distant

they all
become this
same yellow
voiceless
chicken
in the courtyard of
another death
et cetera

thin
sharp thread
which ties
your heart
with one and
the same
relentless
sorrow
of them all

trembling edge-
wise the shadow
of an aspen
leaf through
your eyes
into you

like a platinum
thread
to weigh
stars

constellations
but never
never
your own
heart

*

The same
sea
in us all
red
dark
warm

throbbing
winds from
every quarter
in the sails
of the heart

line
of foam through
white
space

question falling
from the oar
rolling
back
on the wave
fear
behind the darkness

or the same
sea
waiting
for another

*

Big black hedgehog
eternity descending
into the valley

a spiny ball
melting
in the hands
of a child

all
frontiers
barbed wire
of
the world

walking
like hedgehogs
over
all frontiers

children's eyes
resting
like butterflies
at
your feet

*

A flying fish
takes wing
from the book

through the seal
of the Milky Way
on the swell

on the other
side where
the great sea
dissolves
everything
to its primeval
elements

even
death
too little
for this
great
world

*

Ant trail
on a
poplar's
gnarled
trunk

memory
small light
in the damp
cloud

then
between
two worlds
you lose
direction

what pulls
you upward
is it
your weight

what pulls
you down
is it
your wings

not yet grown
yet growing

*

Summer's
last evening
cloudy
and warm

no one
you visited
was at home

two useless
bottles
of wine
in your bag

everyone
you met
in the street
was drunk

everybody
drunk
in the street

     *

So light
after all
this great and
evil world
built
of butterflies'
wings

springtimes
big cities
pestilences
gliding
over history

you
me
who does
need
consolation

fluttering
of motley
wings

caught
by a gust
over
the lake

you too
long ago
cast
your last
glance

said
your last
word

*

Heart
of rain
where nothing
stirs

only the
difference
of black
and white
halving
a random
falling
drop

Nymphalis Io
wings
folded on
the smithy
window

poems
and flames
dying out
in the great
joy
of waters
that meet

in the little
flowing
world
the tears
lose
meaning

*

Ashes
of one world
crumble
upon the colours
of another one

the sunflower
lost
its crown

hoarfrost
on the scythe
grasshoppers
silent

three sheep
in the fog
the rowan tree
stripped
of leaves
and berries

to write
write
something
something
else

*

Painting
a boat
you need not
paint the water

painting
a smile
you need not
paint the face

painting
a blossom
you need not
paint the flower

and you can say
you have to bear
a mote
from the immense
weightlessness
of the world.

*

The late well-master
of Veskimoisa
lives on
unlike the others

In water
in springs

From under
the lid
thrust aside
from the dark square
his sky looks
every day
into your eyes

*

With a broken wing
somebody whisks off
the letters
and breadcrumbs

children are picking up
motley pens
in the courtyard

perhaps it is better
if no one thinks
which were the wings
that bore me once

high above
this strange earth

as snow
as ash
as water

I will come I will flow back
little by little
to everywhere

and when someone
standing on
the roadside will count
kernels from an ear
in his hand or
gather his pockets
full of acorns

no one of them
will ever recognise
me again

*

Everything melts
burns out:
lamp lampshade
the light itself
with no shade left

no world
belongs to you and you
belong
to no world

you are pulled
by rain and light
on roads coming
and going
from everywhere
to everywhere

*

A tit
upside down
picking last seeds
from a frost-bitten sunflower

we came back
bees had abandoned their hives
a dead mouse
was floating in the well

north wind roaming
over dead grass
in our garden
and hillside

at night
we stood long
on the stairs
with the boys
and looked for
Taurus and Aries
rising from the southeast
a rat was hustling
through dead vines

this fall
space for a while
more real than time

*

Ink not yet
dried
loaf of bread
not yet
eaten

spring
come
and gone

colours
growing
again and
again on
my burnt
happy
wings

which do not
know if they
belong to
a philosophy
or
to a butterfly

*

Wiping away
dust
washing away
mud
from the ten
boots
of my family

waiting for snow

time goes
winter goes

     *

Swarms of daws
are flying
home
from the west

black
on the purple background
of the sunset

over the town
depot
over hundreds
of elbowing people
grey in the dusk

who do not know
what to do
with their large
black wings

going home
going to work

*

All in one
one in all
mind in body
body in mind
the strange in the ordinary
the ordinary in the strange
a swarm of bees
in an old chest
in the loft
of an abandoned
farmhouse

*

The white vase
on the white piano
glowing
through the blue
stream of dusk
that carries
me with
myself
with this house
this room
this you

I am ready
to go
to flow
it is good
like remembering
that I
have stored the matches
and firewood
for winter

*

Little by little
our dirty river
flows itself clean
little by little
perhaps we too

manage
to take each other
by hand
back to the endless
purity of
this world
understanding
we have never
really left it

*

Little by little
a poem fades
I dreamt
a poem about
a beautiful girl
on white sand
on the far side
of flashing water

it was written
and read
by someone else
and the longing
to flow like sand
over her legs
belonged to someone else

yours
was only
that dream you could not
be rid of

*

An understanding
of someone
coming nearer
from far off

everywhere
you are
only simply HERE

a pine tree in sea-wind
grey beard of lichen
swinging together
with the twig

    *

I am both
spider and fly
snared in my own
web who sometime
in the evening
thinks
how to reel
into a single ball
all these endless
sticky soul-threads
to throw them
into the blue fire
that sometimes
rises
from the bottom
of my mind
between sleep
and waking

*

Dana paramita
from this
red fragrant strawberry
I brought you
in the evening dusk
coming home after mowing
there remained only
a gentle red glow
we see
we remember
between sleep
and waking
between
two dreams

*

Dana paramita: (Sanskrit) the perfection of charity.

There is nothing
between us
but oblivion

something coming into mind
in your eyes
in your helpless
little hands

I have never existed
never at all

*

To wake
in the dead of night
from sleep
from myself
as I am
as I was
before I was born
no light no darkness
only astonishment
that I am here
and inability
to tell
how it all
really is

before and beyond
the sword-blow
of the great oblivion
that gave you
this time
and space
and name

*

from

THE WANDERING BORDER

(1987)

translated by
JAAN KAPLINSKI
with SAM HAMILL
and RIINA TAMM

The East-West border is always wandering,
sometimes eastward, sometimes west,
and we do not know exactly where it is just now:
in Gaugamela, in the Urals, or maybe in ourselves,
so that one ear, one eye, one nostril, one hand, one foot,
one lung and one testicle or one ovary
is on the one, another on the other side. Only the heart,
only the heart is always on one side:
if we are looking northward, in the West;
if we are looking southward, in the East;
and the mouth doesn't know on behalf of which or both
it has to speak.

*

The washing never gets done.
The furnace never gets heated.
Books never get read.
Life is never completed.
Life is like a ball which one must continually
catch and hit so that it won't fall.
When the fence is repaired at one end,
it collapses at the other. The roof leaks,
the kitchen door won't close, there are cracks in the foundation,
the torn knees of children's pants...
One can't keep everything in mind. The wonder is
that beside all this one can notice
the spring which is so full of everything
continuing in all directions – into evening clouds,
into the redwing's song and into every
drop of dew on every blade of grass in the meadow,
as far as the eye can see, into the dusk.

＊

We started home, my son and I.
Twilight already. The young moon
stood in the western sky and beside it
a single star. I showed them to my son
and explained how the moon should be greeted
and that this star is the moon's servant.
As we neared home, he said
that the moon is far, as far
as that place where we went.
I told him the moon is much, much farther
and reckoned: if one were to walk
ten kilometres each day, it would take
almost a hundred years to reach the moon.
But this was not what he wanted to hear.
The road was already almost dry.
The river was spread on the marsh; ducks and other waterfowl
crowed the beginning of night. The snow's crust
crackled underfoot – it must
have been freezing again. All the houses' windows
were dark. Only in our kitchen
a light shone. Beside our chimney, the shining moon,
and beside the moon, a single star.

*

My little daughter, with both her hands, is strewing
white sawdust on white birchbark.
The wind is blowing from the southwest. Everything
is suddenly so full of this wind
and of this autumn. It is as if
the movement of the clouds has
at last moved something that until now
did not stir, was in blossom, was lush and green. Everywhere
such clarity that oblivion finds no place.
Barberries on thorny twigs.
Nettles near the barn door already yellow.
But the birchbark and the fresh sawdust
under the saw and in the tiny palm of the child
suddenly so much more white and clean than before.

*

To write more. To speak more. To whom?
How? Why? What sense does it make? Soon
we may be forced into silence. Soon
we may be forced to speak more
and more loudly. Who knows. But what
remains unspoken is always the most important:
this little man, this child, this
word, thought, and look of a child
deep inside you, you must guard,
you must defend and cherish.
And with it you will learn to speak,
and with it you will learn to be silent
if you must.

*

On the other side of the window, on the other side of the pylon,
of the dung barrow and snowberry bush,
on the other side of the barn roof where southwest wind
for the third day is scattering ash leaves;
on the other side of the Crincels apple tree,
of the raspberries and of the spruce hedge,
on the other side of the foggy field, of the forest and clouds,
of the autumn, of the sky, of the wind,
on the other side of this life, here,
suddenly, a lone tardy dandelion
unfolds and takes
thoughts from my head and words from my mouth.

*

There is no Good, no Evil, no Sin, no Virtue,
no Faithfulness, no Unfaithfulness, no Marriage, no Adultery.
There is also no Love, although sometimes
these and other words are spoken or written
on paper, on sand, into stone or wind.
There is only the great soul which has
no greatness nor smallness, something
between thoughts and entrails that sometimes starts
as I see you gathering apples under an apple tree
or cutting our little boy's hair or taking
off your nightgown, and I do not know
whether the echo of this beginning will ever end.

*

Four-and-a-half tons of Silesian coal –
a whole day to shovel it into the cellar,
a whole winter to burn it. I'm happy to have it,
and – as always – I regret a little
that I must burn something so wonderful
without having time to study it, to open layer by layer
the book that has been buried and hidden for so long.
I understand almost nothing of these
single lumps that bear distinct
traces of leaves or bark from ancient trees.
Always a book, a black book in a foreign language
from which I understand only some single words:
Cordaites, Bennetites, Sigillaria, Sigillaria...

                    *

Once while carrying coal ash and used paint drums to the dustbin
I remembered it once more: there is
no difference between the common and the strange.
If there is any difference, it is only in ourselves, in our eyes.
For God, it is as common to create or to destroy worlds
as it is for us to write a letter or to read
editorials or the obit page. To himself,
God is no God. To ourselves, we are gods.
In this sense, there is no God. There are
eyes, eyes where a rusty oil barrel takes tender white roots,
and yesterday's newspaper bursts into bloom
and moths swarm around it till dawn.

*

People were coming from the market carrying plum trees;
white lines were being drawn on the asphalt.
Going home, I saw once more
the white tortured trunks of birches
and their foliage breaking out in leaves
and the clouded sky reflected in floodwater pools,
I suddenly felt that this beauty
was becoming almost unsupportable –
it's better to look on ground where charming
tiny burdocks, nettles and mugworts
are coming up
or go indoors and find in the dictionaries
what, after all, are the meanings of Japanese words,
yugen, *sabi*, and *mono-no-aware*:
obscurity, mystery,
and charm or sadness for what is.

*

Sometimes I see so clearly the openness of things.
The teapot has no lid, the colt has no saddle.
Black horses come racing out of memory
carrying young boys on their backs and rush over
the empty steppe and through the haze
through which we see, dimly,
some single peaks…. I too have come from there.
I have something of you, my forefathers,
Amurat, Ahmed, Tokhtash, something of you
black Tartar horses on boundless expanses.
I too do not like to return
to lived life, to an extinguished fire,
to a thought thought to a written poem.
I am burning with the same urge to reach the Atlantic,
to reach the borders always vanishing and breaking
in front of the black horses who again and again
race out from memories and steppes
smelling the west wind that brings from somewhere very far
the odour of the sea and rain.

*

It gets cold in the evening. The sky clears.
The wind dies out, and the smoke
rises straight up. The flowering maple
no longer buzzes. A carp
plops in the pond. An owl hoots twice
in its nest in the ash tree.
The children are asleep. On the stairs,
a long row of shoes and rubber boots.
It happened near Viljandi: an imbecile boy
poured gasoline on the neighbour's three-year-old son
and set him on fire. I ran for milk.
You could see the yellow maple from far off
between the birches and the spruce. The evening star
was shining above the storehouse. The boy survived,
probably maimed for life. The night will bring frost.
Plentiful dew.

*

A piebald cat
sits alone in the middle of the mown field
waiting for something, perhaps a mouse,
perhaps for darkness. We all
wait for the rain. Clouds came and went;
in the morning, it drizzled, but then the wind rose
and raged until noon, drying
even that scant moisture. The village people
grumble that their cattle have hardly anything to eat.
Time moves sideways, looking at this
empty land above which
warm south winds sweep and buzzards
shriek. No longer summer. Nor autumn yet.

*

The early autumn, a faded aquarelle,
becoming more and more colourless and depthless.
Big clumsy flies creeping through window slits
into our rooms, unable to get out again,
as every autumn. From evening to evening,
clouds gather, but there is no dew at night. Jays
pick last peas in the garden.
Thrushes perch in flocks on rowan trees.
Everything seen and known before. The long drought
leaves its traces in our face and mind,
and it is difficult to believe that there is something new
under the sun save the wind and deceptive clouds,
meteor flashes in the night sky and some
chance things you happen to see and remember as with this
earwig that for a long while was turning around
on the gravel path in front of our house.

*

The crop is reaped and mice are coming in from the fields
to the farmhouse, and the owls follow them in.
Sometimes in the evening they call one another
from one corner of the garden to another. I found
a butterfly with worn-out wings in the grass – it could not
fly any more. One night while I went out to pee,
I saw the Milky Way for the first time. A nutcracker
shrieked in the hazel hedge – the nuts are ripe.
The wasps abandoned their nests. They are flying
and feasting, slipping into beehives,
into jam cans and overripe apples;
and grasshoppers are sawing in the grass and on the trees
more and more loudly, and dolorous
as the summer's last string knowing it will break.

*

Poetry is verdant – in spring
it is born from each raindrop, each
ray of light falling on the ground.
How much room do we have for them
between a morning and an evening
or upon a page in a book?
But now, in autumn when black clouds
slide low above us, brushing
high-tension pylons and crows
dozing there in the dusk, because
there is hardly day at all, the night is
two long black fingers holding day
and us in a grip so tight we barely have
room to breathe or think. Everything I write
is in spite of this weight
that comes, comes again, wanting
to plunge us into sleep,
into the dreams of decaying leaves and grassroots
and of the earth itself where
all our unthought thoughts and unborn poems hide.

*

Silence of night. A cockroach
comes out from under the bathtub
in a fifteenth-storey flat; the switch
is out of order, and the lamp
often lights itself.
It climbs up the wall and stops
on the shelf just above the sink. Who knows why.
Perhaps the smell of odours oozing
from bottles, gallipots, and tubes with inscriptions
Wars After Shave Spartacus Sans Soucis Bocage
Arcancil Exotic Intim Desodor Pound's Cream
Cocoa Butter Pond's Dry Skin Cream Maquimat
Avon Chic Privileg Fath de Fath Aramis
Savon Ambre Ancien eau de Cologne...
Perhaps it has an inkling of something
great and mysterious, of a transcendental reality
behind these colourful labels or perhaps
the odours have simply obliterated other traces of smell
from its path leading into the socket hole and from there
into the kitchen behind the breadbox.

*

We always live our childhood again.
Even then, we don't want it back.
Like me. In each year-before-last's memory
is something melancholy and oppressive, probably
war and oppression's shadow from which it was so difficult,
almost impossible to get free, and still
some hazy sadness. I believe that only as a man
have I known joy, and only then,
when I began to write, the mist cleared away
and these shadows. Even from memory,
the essential is born pure:
air, water, earth, trees and houses,
and old walkway slabs on streets in suburbia
poured from concrete or cut from flat, natural stone.
Neither the eyes nor the soles of the feet have forgotten them,
and when I see them again, they are cold and soft
and pedestrians' feet have pressed them still further into a slope
so that with a child's carriage or crutches
it is already difficult to travel
Jaama, Liiva or Tähtvere streets.
What will become of them? Will anyone
make them neatly level again,
or will they be covered with asphalt, and wheels
roll more easily over our childhood
paths and memories.

*

Dialectics is a dialogue, a play of shadows
with somebody darker than darkness
whose eye sees nothing and whose ear hears nothing.
Only sometimes it stretches its hand,
as dark as itself and imperceptibly soft,
and scatters all our cards and pieces,
our formulae, theories, religion and atheism,
and we must begin anew,
until its hand or breath once again
overturns everything
or understand that it is
permanent otherness, nothing but Something Else.

*

Destruktivität ist das Ergebnis ungelebten Lebens.
Destructivity is the result of an unlived life.
What cannot grow up grows down –
nails and hairs of the beard into the flesh, unrequited desires
calcifying our blood vessels, envy
changing into ulcers, sadness into lice,
dirt into flies. We are always,
in a way, wandering knights; we are always looking
for what to fight for and against, whom
to hate with a just hatred. This unlived life
is like a boiling water pot in our hands
which we hurry to put away, and there
is no time for anything else, and we are angry
at all who sit quietly
around the kitchen table and talk
about Erich Fromm and that destructivity
is the result of an unlived life.

*

Elder trees that thrushes have sown
near St Peter's cemetery under the precipice
are bigger and more abundantly flowered
than last year. Some steps farther,
the ruins of a burnt house
are vanishing under burdock and nettles.
In the garden there are always the same
leafless trees – a willow and some apple trees
I tried to draw a year ago
when it was spring, as now, and my mother
was dying in the hospital. The gulls shriek
and boats drone farther up the river.
And in the bushes near the old dump,
the nightingales continue to sing the same
'lazy girl, lazy girl, where's the whip, where's the whip'
as though they had learned nothing
and forgotten nothing.

*

Once I got a postcard from the Fiji Islands
with a picture of sugar-cane harvest. Then I realised
that nothing at all is exotic in itself.
There is no difference between digging potatoes in our Mutiku
    garden
and sugar-cane harvesting in Viti Levu.
Everything that is is very ordinary
or, rather, neither ordinary nor strange.
Far-off lands and foreign peoples are a dream,
a dreaming with open eyes
somebody does not wake from.
It's the same with poetry – seen from afar
it's something special, mysterious, festive,
No, poetry is even less
special than a sugar-cane plantation or potato field.
Poetry is like sawdust coming from under the saw
or soft yellowish shavings from a plane.
Poetry is washing hands in the evening
or a clean handkerchief that my late aunt
never forgot to put in my pocket.

*

Potatoes are dug, ash trees yellow,
sunflower seeds, ripe apples rotting
under the apple tree – as always,
we have more works than days and something
is always left unharvested, unpicked, unfinished.
The plot has to be dug, the fence needs mending –
then we can go, the sky overcast.
Soon, the leaves will be fallen, soon
the essence of things will be more clearly visible:
the black bare twigs of a lowland birch swaying
on the horizon of a grey twilit sky.

*

from

THROUGH THE FOREST

(1991/1996)

translated by
HILDI HAWKINS

There is so little that remains: the handful of last year's snow
that I squeezed in my hand as we skied, the three of us,
towards Kvissental across the peat pond.
The wind in the heather between Vild and Audaku.
The scent of St John's wort and marjoram tea in Arüküla in the
    early morning.
The tit that flew into the stove and was burnt to death.
A couple of folk songs, a wooden spoon,
the cockerel on St John's church and a little piece of black bread,
we do not even know when and where from. What do they have
    in common?
We do not know that, either. Between the great fingers of the
    twilight,
which slowly close tight around us,
a few tiny crumbs sometimes fall. Something of us.
Something of the world. Something that remains undiscovered.
Goes on falling. We do not know where from, we do not know
    where to.

*

To eat a pie and to have it – I
sometimes succeed – I exchange
a piece of lived life for poetry, and then on
for roubles and kopecks – I live off that same
life, eat my own tail and shins
and they grow again, always anew
and the eagle of poetry rises again into flight
and tries to rise with me away from this world
towards a higher world, from which, once,
I was expelled. I remember it
and in my dreams I see it over and over again,
but in reality I do not know how to go there,
although I go on reading stories and folklore studies,
believing that one day I shall discover the way.
Then I shall still need wings. Only wings.
Perhaps my own.

*

Lines do not perhaps exist; there are only points.
Just as there are no constellations, only stars
which we combine into water carriers, fish, rams,
virgins, scorpions and ourselves.
Points are of themselves, lines of us.
Lines are not real. Constellations, contours, profiles,
outlines, ground plans, principles, reasons,
ulterior motives and consequences...
A solitary birch holds onto its last leaves by the woodshed.
Or the leaves hold onto the birch.
Or there is someone who holds onto them both,
like a child holding his father's and mother's hands at once.
I am sorry for them – the child, the leaves, the father, the birch
    and the mother.
But I do not know, really, for whom: if die birch exists,
if there are only points. I do not want the winter.
But I do not know whether the winter really exists. There are
    only points.
There are only molecules and atoms, which move increasingly
    slowly,
which is roughly the same as saying: warmth disperses
throughout space. Both the child's hands were cold.
Night is coming – light is roughly the same as warmth.
Light scatters in the empty room. New thoughts
come so seldom. Your hand is warm. So is the night.
The poem is ready. If the poem exists at all:
there are only points. It is dark.

*

As the night begins, a forked birch captures
the light of a streetlamp and is as bright
as the nameless star that shines between its branches.
The snow remains in darkness, the snow slips the mind,
only the birch does not go, does not stay, and the star
in the dark sky, and the child who slithered
all the way home from school, slid, fell down
and got up again. But the snow slips the mind,
in the snow's place is empty space, but it is perhaps
this which makes breathing so light
and the sky so deep.

*

I begin to wash my son's shirt. In the pocket I find a piece of paper.
On it:

2: 06 27

An hour ago winter began. Now we are speeding towards
summer at 30 km/s. The sun is reflected in the window.

The washing is done. I come out. Under the Christmas tree, all
the children's animals are gathered in bunches: the tiger, the
lion, six dogs, two bears, a squirrel, a beaver, two cats, a lizard
and someone else besides.

Just as in the prophecy of Isaiah, in which 'the wolf shall dwell
with the lamb, and the lion shall eat straw like the ox'.

I would then eat fresh bread and grapes.

Fresh bread and grapes, and in the evenings a little garlic.

What is the weather like now in Palestine? What is in flower there
now?

I go to catch the bus. I stand by the roadside beside the hawthorn
hedge and break off a

long thorn.

As a toothpick.

There are still a few frozen berries on the bush.

*

Think back to the vanished day
from which you are separated by sleep, restless, erotic.
Think, remember, find yesterday's own face,
so that you will not be lost in oblivion, will not be lost
among similar faces, amid time
that has passed only in activity,
walking, talking, searching the shops for
a jacket or a desk, getting angry because
the table is so difficult to put together,
some bolts are damaged and there are none
in reserve – economic policy at screw level,
since at the same time metal is simply dug into the ground
by the ton – all of this creates
a background of irritation to the everyday, just like clouds,
through which so few things can reach,
a fresh thought, a fresh glance, a woman's or a child's
laugh, you note what gives even the day
most of the way it looks – the look of a living person,
you make contact, you are together, you draw
with a coloured pencil, Lemmit and Elo-Mall
draw too and when they ask what is it
you're drawing you say, oh, nothing much.

*

Once, at a meeting, I was asked
to describe a poet's day. So
I did:

> I get up and make porridge for the children.
> I take one child to school or study at home with the other.
> I take the other child to school.
> I go to the grocer's shop.
> I meet some friends in the town.
> I talk on the telephone at home.
> I do the laundry.
> I clean the room.
> I read a newspaper.
> I write a little.
> I make food for someone.
> I eat.
> I put one child in the bath and then settle it for sleep.
> I make the bed.
> I lie down.
> I discuss the day's news with my wife.
> If I am not very tired, I read.
>
> . . . .

It was like this, or a little different.
It is like this, or a little different.

*

Death does not come from outside. Death is within.
Born-grows together with us.
Goes with us to kindergarten and school.
Learns with us to read and count.
Goes sledging with us, and to the pictures.
Seeks with us the meaning of life.
Tries to make sense with us of Einstein and Wiener.
Makes with us our first sexual contacts.
Marries, bears children, quarrels, makes up.
Separates, or perhaps not, with us.
Goes to work, goes to the doctor, goes camping,
to the convalescent home and the sanatorium. Grows old,
sees children married, retired,
looks after grandchildren, grows ill, dies
with us. Let us not fear, then. Our death
will not outlive us.

*

The wind does not blow. The wind is the process of blowing itself.
Can there be wind that does not blow? Sun that does not shine?
A river that does not flow? Time that does not flow.
For time is flux. But no one knows what it is that
flows. Or can there suddenly be
time that waits, that remains in one place like the lake
behind the dam? Can there be fire that has not yet
begun to burn, that has not even begun to glow?
Can fire be cold? Can lightning not yet have struck?
Thoughts not yet be thought? Can there be life
that is not yet lived and will perhaps remain
an empty space, a black hole in a dry witches'-broom,
a wave that freezes before it reaches the shore and now
gazes at me from the edge of the table
and knocks at my heart in my sleep?

*

You step into the morning, which every day grows
darker and darker. Two silent shapes
disappearing into the garage – the last I see of you.
Sleep will no longer come. The radio is playing music
which is as grey as the weekday morning.
Now you have already driven off, now turned on the headlights,
now you begin to move, reach the main road,
to flow with the sparkling flow of cars going to work and school,
you disappear beyond a curve and all that remains of you
is an image and belief and trust that you will come back,
and love, which may be greater yet,
still greater perhaps than the dark grey which is becoming light grey
in the yard, in the house, and in us.

*

The ticking of the clock fills the room.
Time conquers the room. Time and darkness,
in which you hear your own breathing, your eye-
lids' untiring open-shut, open-shut
and – more than you would think – the beating of your heart,
life's own biological clock, lub-dub, which is much older
than tick-tock, much closer to time itself,
time, which perhaps, really,
is something more than ticks and tocks,
is the voice of someone who has for two billion years
been wanting to say something to you, to life or to matter.
Perhaps this is the answer, one letter,
one syllable in an answer which, after two billion years,
is about to be completed.

*

A flock of jackdaws on the outskirts of the town – in the twilight
fluttering hither and thither in the wind and rain,
tearing apart like an old grey tea-towel,
a cloth forgotten in the washing-place in the yard
where in the rain, snow and sun
it slowly rotted, moved from the man-made world back into nature
and in the spring, when we tried to wipe our hands on it
it fell into shreds on the sprouting grass.
It, too, returns, only in a different form, as something else
and it is much more difficult to recognise than the grey birds
that, each evening, fly to the trees in the graveyard for the night
and, each morning, fly to the town and to the dumping ground
and one day, too, will decompose and meet
the old tea-towel and last year's newspapers,
tin crowns from the Estonian time, Rinaldo Rinaldini and Tarzan,
me and you and all the encounters, passings-by,
which can somehow take on the appearance of you and me and
        the flock of jackdaws
and the tea-towel and the tin crown and the twilight.

*

I do not write, do not make poetry, about summer, about autumn,
about winter or about spring, about nature or about people.
I write about writing, about making poetry itself.
I am writing a poem, although I don't know how,
I really don't – if I did, I would do it all the time,
I would know beforehand what I will write, but I don't know.
    What comes, comes,
and sometimes does not come at all. I don't know what it is
what (or who) brings to mind its beginning,
whether bird or butterfly, woman or child or word,
something you notice and see more clearly than at other times.
That I don't know how to do either, sometimes it simply works,
I can't direct my own eyes or mind, I don't know
who or what directs them. What directs noticing,
understanding. If there's something I can do, perhaps it's
observing that observation, grasping that seeing.
If that's knowledge; perhaps it's the opposite.
Perhaps, after all, poetry comes entirely from ignorance,
is a particular sort of ignorance. And that
is much harder to learn than knowing.

*

I never weary of looking at leafless trees. Poplars,
lindens, birches – everything that can be seen
from my window. I do not know what it is in them that is at once
so strange and intolerably beautiful, so that I always want
to do something, want to draw them,
or describe them, although I do not know how.
I do not know, either, how to describe what I feel
as I sit at the window and watch the swaying of the branches
in the growing twilight, a few crows
in the top of the old ash, the birch in front of the woodshed.
I simply write about them, name them:
Populus, Tilia, Betula, Ulmus, Fraxinus,
as some read mantras, some name saints.
And I feel better. Perhaps I even know
that in those treetops, branches, in that ordinary,
windy pattern, drawn in black on grey,
is something much more. As in the hollow of one's hand:
Nature. Fate. The future. The poplars character.
The birch's fate. The lindens temperament. It is very hard
to explain in words. Without words
it is hardly easier. The worlds of people
and of trees are so different. But still,
there is something so human, almost intelligible,
in that tangle of branches. It is like a script,
like a language that I do not understand, although I know
that what is written there
has long been known to me; it cannot be much different
from what can be read in books,
hands or faces.

*

The most disconsolate of landscapes – a beach in autumn,
leafless brushwood, full of scraps of plastic, tin cans, condoms.
Lopsided changing rooms, a crow's tracks
by the water's edge on the wet sand, snails' shells,
leafless branches, sodden roots
and everywhere the low low sky and clouds
rushing as if they were in a hurry
to get somewhere far away before the dark,
which has never really disappeared, which is always
in the same place between the bushes, billowing before your eyes,
eyeing you; which presses on your temples
like a damp hand. And still, in all this,
there is so much unintelligible light, and you cannot tell
whether it is shining from the outside in, or the inside out,
whether it is white or black or something completely different.

*

Silence. Dust

1

In the beginning is no beginning.

In the beginning is silence. Silence is within you. You dare not
touch it prematurely – no one dares.

It is not worth being a 'poet' – writing poems, unless you cannot
do otherwise – if you can, leave them unwritten.

Silence and light.

Bright silence, beneath which those words exist. Images. Pictures.
Poetry.

Mouse nests. Spiders. Ticks. Queen bees. Clumps of grass.

The world under the clumps.

Albrecht Dürer and Harry Martinson. Dreaming forever of what
they saw,

from which they got their picture or poetry. A clump with violets.
Clumps – *Tuvor.*

Artist and poet hibernating in their own creation,

covered by written and unwritten pages.

Yet paper remains white rather than mottled, patterned, written
upon.

Individual letters are like freckles, they don't change anything much.

The bright silence remains. Snow, and beneath the snow, ice, and
under the ice a current, quivering, arrowheads and spring moss.

Mouse tracks in the snow, which the wind wipes away. Snow dust
spinning

over the emptiness, a couple of milkweed leaves and pieces of
pine bark.

A couple of words. Laconic, far eastern, almost wordless
wordsmanship.

White silence. An actor's white make-up, beneath which, deep in
the darkness, the face and the soul with their own passions.

A throaty song, a song that comes from the stomach, from a person's
centrepoint, his deepest part, his Marianas trench.

2

Wherever there is silence, dust gathers.

Dust wants peace. Dust gathers where there is little movement. Dust comes

from near and far, from roads, ploughs, old fur coats, volcanoes and outer space.

Dust comes and settles on piano lids in arts centres, old Bibles in attics, shelves, rugs, laundries, smithies, abandoned mills,

in old outbuildings where old wooden bowls stand, yarn windles, dismantled looms and chests full of balls of rags.

I, too, want peace. That is why I encounter dust so often.

I love to visit laundries, smithies, abandoned mills and old outhouses.

I believe that time moves more slowly there, and thoughts or images or whatever one should call them sink in slower time slowly to the ground.

Sometimes onto this paper here, and so sometimes they can be called writing, a text.

Before time breaks in the doors and something remains hopelessly unfinished,

the castle in the air unbuilt, the train of thought unspun, the mind unclarified.

Only over paper does time not have great power.

Sometimes something remains there.

Like, for example:

3

Peace conquers everything.
Peace hoists the flag of peace
over chimney, sauna, garden,
campfires, Pond Hill,
where once the Southern and Northern Kingdoms
waged war all summer long.

All is full of peace,
car, outbuilding, sauna, shed, byre, privy,

beehives, nesting-boxes, bath, washbasin,
ash bucket, wheelbarrow, flowerpots, paint tins,
baskets, barrels, pockets and plates.

My own disquiet no longer
finds a place to be,
there is no longer room for it anywhere
except in words;
my restlessness can
now exist only
in heart and poetry.

Poetry is an extension of the heart,
an extension of its beating
into trees, bushes,
apple blossom, scarlet grosbeaks,
spider's thread, clotheslines.

4

PEACE
is when everything slowly grows its roots,
this old outbuilding, this greenhouse,
this rhubarb clump, which I planted the day before yesterday,
this old iron, this old samovar,
those little vases Tiia made,
this empty matchbox,
this figure carved from limewood,
this pebble, brought from Saaremaa, full of fossilised snails' shells,
this *kantele*, which we found in an empty house,
this little mouse, which runs under the loom from one wall to the
    other,
this spider, which waits on the dusty windowpane,
this old, white button on the windowsill,
this fork, which came to light as we dug the garden,
these apple trees, those garden posts, those laths, those trellises,
those wall logs, dead these sixty years,

those shingles, which we cut at the Sahkri sawmill –
all these are gradually growing roots.
I, too.

5

The spider has sucked dry
one more fly
Life-sap changes owner.
The affinity of everything for everything,
the war of everything against everything,
the great festival of creation
in which everything is, in turn,
the eater and the eaten
and what succeeds in escaping
sinks into the sand or the mire
and eventually becomes coal
and instead of burning
in someone's innards
it burns in a central heating furnace
one February afternoon,
when the tit sings for the first time
and the red sun begins to set
in the southwest behind the radar and the forest.

6

The white wagtail flies
in the wind to the swaying wire,
finds its balance
and sings its brief, passionate song.
The rain has stopped for a moment,
only
here and there, from the leaves of an apple tree,
a few drops fall and, caught by a drop,
a few white petals fall
down onto the black peat heap.

7

The cuckoo, the clock of springtime,
behind the marsh in the birch grove:
tick-tock
cuck-oo
strikes, as if with an axe,
shavings from the side of time.
My son makes a boat
and cuts his finger again.
The drop of blood marks
the present moment,
the moment of free fall
when all are equal –
the stone and the feather,
the beggar and the king,
the gnat and the poet,
the yarn windle and the bootjack.
The future – a great black hole
in a black void.
I do not see it,
do not feel its weight.

8

The rain is like the centipede
who began to think
how it is he walked
and could not continue his journey.

Again and again the drops fall
onto the same
flowers, leaves, twigs,
but the sun moves on
somewhere in the upper air.

Looms and shadows
stand still,

the spider in its net-corner
and the whistle in the mouth of the warbler.
Only thought moves
and the gooseberries swell
against the autumn
which one can still say is
far off.

It is good that one's eyes
do not look backward
inside oneself
and that grey hairs
are no heavier to bear
than black ones.

9

Three spiders
have divided between them
the four panes of the window,

the transparent landscape,
in whose background
in the third dimension
the apple tree blossoms
and the leaves of the snowberry
palpitate under the rain-
drops.

On the windowsill
a pair of dried wings.
One dried butterfly.

10

On the other side of the garden, behind the streaming rain,
on the wall of the room
tick the grandfather clock and the electricity meter,
never catching each other up.

The radio is still playing
Schubert's unfinished symphony,
the voice of the rain fills the pauses,
the silence the voice of the rain.
No one knows where they come from.
No one knows where they go.

But we are ourselves
differently from music,
differently from the rain.
For we do not, really, live –
life lives in us
like fire in a burning field
leaping from stem to stem.

Perhaps somewhere someone
is turning a cornfield into an assart,
sowing seeds in the ashes.
But that
is already beyond my understanding.

11

What, after all, can I write?
About what was – memories.
About what could come to be – dreams.

I do not want either.
I want to write
above all about what is.

About the present. But the present is
the meeting of two walls – the very same
memories and dreams. And between them
is only a corner, too tight
to write in it, *it is*.

Now I understand:
I stand once more in the corner
as once in University Street
and want to believe that from there
from that elusive hue
a door opens to somewhere else
somewhere far away.

12

When you write, you have died a little.
If you want to write about life
it is difficult to grasp it
and live.
You have stepped away from life:
instead of living, you write;
if you want to be honest,
you must write about writing,
about how you write instead of living,
about how you write about
how you write instead of living,
the same again here, the same again
about the same again.
You want to draw a line through everything
which would lead to that same
nonexistent present
point.
In the belief that through the point
passes yet another line, the door to
the other side.

In the old outbuilding
where I sit at an old table
and where there is suddenly
so much silence and space.

13

Go, go, says the easing rain.
Away, away, says the easing rain.
A petal from the apple tree falls onto the grass.
Beauty cuts deeply like a knife,
cuts the personality into many pieces.
One self thinks suddenly of November,
of the first snow, which is
like an old lady's clean white net curtain,
only on the other side of the window.
A second self thinks of tiredness,
of how the garden is tired, the house is tired,
the bushes are tired, the flowerbeds are tired,
you yourself are tired, tired of life, existence,
expectation, of getting up and going
into that tired world.
But a third self suddenly realises:
sometimes one can also grow tired of being tired.

When I open the door, raindrops are no longer
falling from the sky. In the southwest the sun glimmers
through a thin cloud. Water drips from the eaves,
but one large bee
is already spinning out from under the outhouse eaves.
I put on my rubber boots and realise
that the world is at the same time
very old and very young
and I myself am neither.

*

The Forest Floor

1

The wind blows high above.
Below, under the birch trees and the raspberry canes
the dusk grows gradually
from which anonymous birds
launch into flight
and disappear into the thicket.

The summer builds, in the timber frame,
a multistoreyed postmodern house
whose inhabitants
do not really know one another.

Seldom does he who lives under the tussock
meet the resident of the tree top.
The ecological thread
which binds everything to everything else
is too long
and too fine.

You come here – you are a stranger.
Here, different laws and relationships hold good.
We may have christened them, but that does not concern them,
they do not know it.
Linnaea borealis knows nothing of Carolus Linnaeus.
It just grows.

Three pine trees, grown together.
You lean against one of them – the trunk is still warm.
The cooling of the air has not yet reached them,
although the stones are already chilled.

A solitary, sickly, congealing gnat
takes its opportunity and lands on the back of your hand.

2

A pile of stones.

Slowly covered by twigs, leaves and moss, until all that is left of it is a mound.

Each stone has its own face, its own colour.

Perhaps they have names and personalities, too, but they are so slow.

Perhaps 11,000 years – about how long it is since the retreating glacier left them here – is not enough for them to gain a clear idea of their identity, to realise their own individuality, their separation from the grey womb of the Northlands from which they were once pulled forth.

We may say we are one with creation, but do we really understand what it means.

We are intruders here, we are very far from those who are at home here.

Like the wood horsetail, which spreads its soft sunshade over the rotting leaves.

Like the wood sorrel, whose flowers are as sour as its leaves.

Like the bilberry, which by springtime has forgotten everything, whose young naïve sprigs are full of optimism and curiosity.

Like the lingonberry – dark and solemn, Juhan Liiv-like, Paul-Eerik Rummo-like, which remembers everything and dares not rise too high,

the lingonberry, the real master, who moves to the forest when the forest is ready.

But *Linnaea*, the twinflower, has begun to move.

I guessed it long ago, I noticed it first.

The twinflower is enlarging its territory, it advances about half a metre a year.

Perhaps its speed will gradually grow – I do not know.

In any case, it has plenty of time, and it will be difficult for anyone to try to keep it from advancing.

I believe it intends to conquer the whole world – which perhaps does indeed belong to it.

3

For a couple of days we all ate young spruce tips, so that our mouths became tender.

And so the summer is at hand.

On the road, by the ditch, a couple of burnt stones from our sauna have crumbled to sand.

On the path grow rushes: a couple of patches of dark, stiff green – like pieces of old horsehair mattress.

At the edge of the forest, in the middle of a footpath, a solitary strawberry blooms, its flower turned towards the south, towards the sun and the open country.

In the dike a stream murmurs and grows spring moss.

Around the forked birch is grass, full of cowslips, like brass key-blanks in a locksmith's drawer.

Which is the true key of the sky?

Blue moor grass and bird's-eye primroses together, as if they were well acquainted with the work of Lippmaa and others on plant association in Estonia.

Amid the ruins of a hay barn between the nettles and the meadowsweet, a solitary dandelion blooms, this year for the first time.

Beauty scratches, like a puppy at a door – when it gets out, it wants in, when it gets in, it wants out –

so that it no longer knows which side it is on,

does not know which is the most painful and essential of all,

the yearning to see it all to the core, to crawl free of oneself, to crumble to dust in all those sky-keys, bird's-eye primroses, rushes, nettles and dandelions

or to scoop them together, whether in photographs, poems or memories, store them up, pass them on to someone who is in need of them

and feel how he begins to come alive again,

to sense the scent of young nettles and streams and the touch of the evening breeze

as I step over the river marsh towards the forest.

*

Dust. I Myself

I, too, was born of the longing of dust.
Dust wants to live.
Dust wants to dance, sing, dust wants eyes, a mouth, backbone and
    intestines, dust wants to speak of its longing for life and light,
of how it is weary of being dust.
Dust speaks and whimpers even as dust, but its words and voice,
    too, are merely dust,
so that it is difficult for us to say which is which.
Which is dust, which voice, which yearning,
which am I, which are we.

Am I a speck of dust or its voice, another speck of dust?
A speck of dust, or its longing to be something else?
Am I silence or voice, dust's silence or its voice,
which contains everything from Gilgamesh to the sorrows of
    young Werther?
From Gilgamesh, who wanted to know Earth's law,
although he who comes to know Earth's law is left weeping on the
    ground.
Enkidu, who was already dust once more, spoke to him:
'Did you see him whom the mast killed?' 'I saw him,
he is under the earth and is dragging forth posts.'
'Did you see him who died…?' 'I saw him,
he sleeps in the bed of night and drinks fresh water.'
'Did you see him who was killed in battle?' 'I saw him;
his father and mother comfort him
and his wife bends over him.'
'Did you see him whose body was thrown on to the wasteland?'
    'I saw him;
his soul beneath the Earth does not rest in peace.'
'Did you see him whose soul is not honoured?' 'I saw him;
he eats scrapings from the pot and crumbs of bread
which have been thrown into the street.'

2

But you, spermatozoon, semen.

You, too, received your longing from somewhere, your longing for the warm, dark primal fluid

in which your, my, our ancestors, once swam, divided, and united again.

The sea. *Thalassa. Thalatta.*

The sea, of which so little now remains.

Sometimes it is memory, sometimes our own blood.

Sometimes sea water, which in Norway during the war was used

for blood transfusions, when there was not enough blood.

Sometimes it is a warm, salty source in a woman's, *your* body, in which once again the miracle of union recurs.

You sense something, like a thread, a cord along which Cambrian, Jurassic, Tertiary, earlier centuries send their messages to future times which do not yet have names,

to countries, kingdoms which do not yet have names.

To peoples who speak languages which do not yet have names.

You are on your way there, sperm, chromosomes, tiny egoistical gene.

I believe that you are a message – then I am the commentary of that message, its translation into flesh and blood – take, eat – only I do not know what it means.

If anything at all.

But does the fact that it means anything or nothing itself mean anything?

Let us think of the sea. And that there is something greater than all questions.

Something that reaches over all borders.

Water, foam, stones, sand.

Wind.

Sometimes warm, sometimes cold.

3

We do not often think that we, too, are written
and that in that which we write there is actually less of ourselves
than of others.
Ancestors, genes, heard, seen and read.
We are variations on a theme which first resounded in some primal
fluid, the theme *life, life.*
It would be easy to believe that in us this theme is heard most
clearly, most perfectly and most beautifully.
But it is hard for me to believe it.
Too much have I watched birds, identified plants and planted trees
and read in nature books strange tales of insects, spiders,
cephalopods and birds.
I recall the bowerbird, which builds a cabin for its wedding
festivities and dyes it with berry-juices.
I recall the spider, which places a spot of glue on the end of a
thread and uses it, like the gaucho his bola, to catch its prey.
I recall the termite and the ant, which in their hollow,
subterranean nests grow mushrooms for their nourishment.
I recall something of the language of the dolphin and the bee, the
beaver's dam-building, the elephant which touches the skull
of a dead elephant with its trunk.
And many, many others, and when I think also of what we have
done to all of them,
when I think of safaris, whale hunters, birds dying of oil pollution
and poisoned rivers
it is difficult, almost impossible for me to believe that we are the
most beautiful voice in the world's music.
Yes, perhaps the *Kalevala*, perhaps the song of Gilgamesh,
perhaps Mozart, perhaps Norbert Wiener,
perhaps gloves from Muhu or the song of the Chukchi.
But there are so few of them, there are in the world impossibly
few people
who are able to make anything really beautiful, and there are ever
fewer of them.

I fear that most of us are a badly played tune, a rattling, a rumbling,
   noise which is gradually extinguishing the great music of life.
We are a part of life that smashes the whole, teeth that gnaw the
   breast, a hand that breaks the fingers of another hand.
For teeth cannot bite themselves, fingers cannot break themselves.
One can destroy oneself only when there is still something.
The universe cannot destroy itself.
An accidental phrase, an accidental comfort,

4

But then: is the noise merely a noise, or does it conceal something
   more?
Do we not play (or is there not played on us) a completely
   different music, cosmic and divine?
For dust has its own dust, and dust's dust its own: in moving
   from great to small we meet, in turn, order and chaos, and
   finally arrive at atoms and even smaller particles, in which all
   is once again, in its own way, regular.
Perhaps the music of the spheres lives yet in the music of the
   electrons and elementary particles – for it exists also in us, in
   our bodies.
But we do not have much in common with our atoms – we live
   on the outer surfaces of our bodies, without reaching the
   depths, we are like slicks of oil on the water's surface.
And the atoms within us are unconscious that we are we (if we
   are!), that they are part of a person, a knife, a daffodil or a
   stone in a field.
But in their world there is no life or death, either; they do
not notice how inanimate material becomes animate, or vice versa.
   We live so much higher than ourselves, we live above our
own heads.
   We are like wind and clouds, like a folk tale or like the gods
in heaven.
   We may live by the light of our own words and myths, in our
own philosophies and castles in the air.

Until they come to fetch us and we fall down into this dusty middle world. (Perhaps there is no dust in heaven, and that makes heaven heaven.)

And we do not understand, either here or there, whether we are noise or music, and if music, then what kind of music.

Or what folk tale, what dream, what existence – questions that do not receive an answer even as we fall for the last time, as our own dust mixes with other dust, but *we ourselves? We ourselves?*

*

To fight for the rights and freedoms of the body,
for arms and legs, mouths and eyes, lungs and livers,
for brains, inner ears and outer ears,
for sex glands and sweat glands, nails and hair,
whom we mercilessly exploit,
whom we force to work for our own good, day and night,
whom we do not allow to live their own lives,
choose their partners or beget offspring according to their own
    wishes.
We subordinate the limbs to the brain and force the brain
instead of interesting thoughts, to think about food and sex,
to imagine stupid fancies, to dwell on our
feelings of inferiority, hypochondria and jealousy
and to govern the other parts of the body. Even in sleep
it is not free of our worries or complexes.
And like a Viking prince, who was buried with
his horses, his women and his servants,
we force our own enslaved parts of the body
to die with us. Only our nails and hair
can, for a few days, grow freely but they, too,
hardly know what to do
with this sudden and brief freedom.

*

This autumn's great big yellow chrysanthemum,
it does not flower; it is Flowering itself,
which in it receives the form of a flower, which is a flower.
Just as the girl whom we meet on Vanemuine hill
is Meeting in the form of the girl,
just as the moon is Shining as moon
and I myself am
Coming Home from School with Child
as Jaan and Lemmit. Only I do not know
what/who expresses itself in language, in this language
which has two heads. If you turn it round,
it begins to spawn Ideas and Gods,
splits us and our everyday affairs
into a playground for the heavenly host,
shadows on the cave wall, which for some reason believe
that the subject must be more real than the predicate
or the other way round. Although I have known
what is real: the stones which the boys threw
at the old saucepan in the yard. And the grapevines
around the veranda. Sometimes the spring sky. Sometimes dreams.

*

Birch tops like brushes
paint the dark darker, the light lighter;
paint dark on darkness,
light on light.
The light remains the thinner:
the tattered shirt of the tattered year.
The gleam of bare skin – it is neither
darkness nor light,
this nor that.
I do not know what it is.
I do not know what I know and do not know.
I do not even know what the sparse
black brushes of the birch branches
write, paint on the dark clouds,
of themselves, of their present,
which has gone, which exists
no longer even as I see it,
when the light from between those branches
has reached my eyes and mind.
For we see only a lost world,
only what is no longer.

*

The beginning of the year is like a white sheet of paper. There has been a snowstorm during the night. I go out to beat the carpets. It is midday, but my footprints are the first outside the house. Perhaps something has happened, but nothing has yet reached us.

Like the sound of an axe-blow from the other side of the river.

Like the light of a new star from somewhere that is called 'above'. Although the sky is on every side: above, below, beside, behind and in front.

Here, too, as I have thought and spoken. And think and speak now, too. In the snowy sky. On the snowy ground. As life stands still like a clock that one has forgotten to wind.

The children are still sleeping after New Year's Eve.

The sheet of paper is still white. Silence is still silence.

The cloud is consoling to watch. Always.

*

Politics and politicians are gradually becoming streamlined, and in their streamlining uniform

like the newest cars, so similar that one has to look at what is written on the back to be certain which is a Toyota, which a Fiat, which a Ford, which a Renault.

Their wind resistance is always decreasing; headlights, windscreen wipers, aerials, door handles, principles and thoughts are concealed by the bodywork, which sinks, closer to the ground,

consumes less petrol per 100 kilometres, weighs less and can, at the speed limit and without leaving traces or memories, race through the community, whose resistance and turbulence have been thoroughly examined on the test circuit.

*

I ended up in literature because it seems, perhaps, closest to my proper place. But what is that proper place? It is that for which I seek, and do not find, a name. In fact, it may be that I do not seek it any longer, but seek instead the possibility of explaining to others that that place, that pigeonhole, does not really exist. It would be to compose poetry without being a poet; to write without being a writer; to philosophise without being a philosopher; to serve Christ without being a Christian; to serve Buddha without being a Buddhist; to express oneself without oneself being anyone.

Nouns are like ice and snow; in them is death and eternity, which are almost the same. Cold, icy, marmoreal eternity. Beauty, with a Capital Letter. Classical sculpture, which is now being destroyed, not by Christians and Muslims, but by the city air, that same city air which once made people free. I sometimes dream of a language in which there are no nouns, only verbs. A thought that may occur more easily to someone who knows the Finno-Ugrian languages, in which even negation is a verb. Like a remainder of an earlier living, changing and flowing world that gradually congeals, freezes into nouns, fossils, ice, theories, principles, and to which you try, more and more desperately and more and more resignedly, to speak of its own youth, of light, which is a flowing and a surging, and of life, which is light.

Behind the window, snow is falling, although it will soon be May; on the slope there are snowdrifts, and on a patch of ground that has been cleared of snow, numb with cold, robins and hedge-sparrows peck at oatflakes. At the same time terribly close and terribly distant. The gaze of the robin's black eye will reach me perhaps only when I, never mind the robin, no longer exist. Perhaps my gaze will also reach him, but it is not certain. For the present, I shall try to speak in words. To speak of life, which cannot be contained in words, which cannot be explained or understood, which can only be lived, and perhaps also protected, like this robin, which is watching me, head tilted, from the top of the little pine, from a couple of decades of light years, or life years – life is the light of men – away.

*

I came from the town. I fetched some cucumber and flower seedlings from my neighbour; put the flowers into the larder to keep cool; planted the cucumbers and sowed some pepper seeds I had brought from the town in the greenhouse, watered them, cut the flourishing grass, nettles and dandelions from around the young apple trees; and then felt sweaty and tired, went down to the lake, took off my clothes and swam. The weather was hot, nearly 25°. I sat, naked, on a bench for a moment and listened to the nightingales. We have not had any for many years, but now, by the lake, where the great weeping willows and bird cherries grow, one had appeared, which, unperturbed by either me or the daylight, did nothing but warble, chuck and gurgle – clearly a great talent among its kind. Then my glance fell on the bird-cherry blossoms which covered the ground around the bench. This year there had not been the usual cold spell when the bird-cherry flowered. I thought about this, and suddenly there came to my mind something which I had noticed, but which was waiting somewhere on the borders of consciousness for further attention: earlier, when I had been speaking with the neighbour's wife, there had been some bird-cherry blossom in her hair. Now that I had dealt with it, I began to feel better: one fact would leave me in peace, would no longer demand a reaction. We had met, I had nodded to it, clearly I was no longer of any use to it. The bird-cherry blossoms simply let me go. But they were not, and are not, definitely alone. Definitely, my mind is full of such impressions and notes awaiting and demanding attention. It is as if an alarm bell were constantly ringing somewhere, you are restless, without yourself knowing why; you have simply forgotten, perhaps deliberately, perhaps accidentally, the queue of unconscious things behind the doors of your consciousness.

*

Autumn comes closer. Everything drowns in yellow.
Golden rod and dahlia. For many months
you had lost your voice; now you begin to chime
more purely and more clearly. In a minor key.
And the yellow, the yellow is every day
fuller of bees, flies and remembrance
of childhood gardens in Tartu and Pärnu,
which were just as languid, luxuriant and damp
and full of the same stillness
in which grasshoppers play music with your soul
and the great hawk-moth, which you find
each morning under the well cover,
knocks each night at the window,
longing to come closer to the lamp
by whose light you sit and write
and think that in autumn borders begin to disappear
leaving moods and colours
leaving the yellow, the yellow...

*

I come up from the cellar: suddenly everything is full of light.

The light greets everything, greets the flower-vase and smiles at it, greets the teddy bear, me and the torch high on the shelf.

The light caresses the backs of all the books at once and shines on all the specks of dust at once, and the dust begins to dance.

The light reminds us, all us specks of dust, that redemption is the understanding that you are redeemed; understanding is the understanding that you have not understood.

Is not and *is* – between them runs the thinnest of thin lines: it has no thickness, no colour, no smell or weight.

Through it? But that is the same as if nothing happened. The spot of sunlight on the wall reaches the seam between two pieces of wallpaper and the cherry petal comes loose from the blossom and begins to fall, continues falling;

for us, in our time, it will never reach the ground, will never find redemption, will never decay .

But in its own time it reaches the floor, finds redemption and understanding.

Is there a third time, something outside past and future (it is not the present, the present is nothing but the border between them), which unites it and our own time, understanding, decay and redemption,

which for a moment wipes away the line between *is not* and *is* like the light whose smile set the dust in the room dancing?

*

A bird in the air. It is not its wings that bear its wings. Its wings are borne by the air. Words stand on wordlessness, logic on the absence of logic.

But sometimes we are, after all, closer to what exists. Before there is something that is like a blanket on top of one who sleeps. The body is unknown, but the blanket has its own folds, bumps and hollows.

We know someone is there beneath the blanket, but that 'someone' and that 'knowing' and that 'we' are even more under wraps than what is under the blanket. We are the blanket, not the sleeper.

We do not know whether he is alive or dead, although from time to time it looks as if he is breathing. And a blanket cannot breathe.

So it is not all the same, after all; all is not a game. But playing is allowed under the blanket, too – hide-and-seek, and make-believe that you are a badger in its sett or a fox in its lair.

I try to speak of this. Always. To think. Sleeping and waking. But my voice resounds as though from deep underwater, and nothing reaches the surface but bubbles.

Truth itself is also a bubble, which you build laboriously there beneath the waters surface, like a water spider, which builds itself a nest and drags air into it, bubble by bubble.

The nest looks like a little silver ball, like a globule of quicksilver, at once so heavy and so agile.

Truth is a bubble, part of the Truth which saves us from suffocating. Truth is that which breathes, and allows others to breathe.

*

In the room, a moth flies from east to west: here inside, too, east and west exist, in the room, in the matchbox and the eye of the needle.

A child throws an orange pip at the window. Bicycles – big and small – lie in each other's embrace in the year's last snow, the year's last freedom,

in which mirrors make themselves transparent, traversable as rooms

in which bricks become mirrors in which you see
the moth's shadow on your face,

which looks, like the god Janus, at once to east and west, forward and back, and sees the orange-pip at once falling and rising.

*

In the ventilation grating lives a tit.

Couperin lives at this moment on the gramophone.

Tadpoles are already living in the pond.

Above the pond, at evening, is a mist, and in the mist live
    nightingales.

As long as they are there, as they come back in springtime,

there is still order and hope in the world, there are still the frail
    threads of migration paths

that connect us with Egypt, Sudan, the Congo, and Cape Province.

The world is still in place, like a map-mosaic, a children's puzzle,
    a jigsaw,

that is so hard to put together and so easy to break up.

My greatest fear is, indeed, perhaps that the time will come when
    some of the pieces of the mosaic will disappear:

the nightingales will not come, the dung-beetle will not fly, and it
    will no longer be possible to put the world together again.

It will remain a confused, half-finished ecological puzzle:

a solitary tit will sing, but will not find a mate.

In the ocean the male blue whale will no longer find his partner.

The continents will break up into islets, skerries, stones
    surrounded by water.

Mankind will break up into parties, classes, principles, homos and
    sapiens,

naked apes which fear serpents, the dark, knowledge and other
    such things

and cower each by his own swaying coconut palm, trying to piece
    together his own map of the stars,

which scatters into the mist like everything else.

The tit came back again. The nightingale is singing.

*

142

from

EVENING BRINGS
EVERYTHING BACK

(1984/2004)

translated by
JAAN KAPLINSKI
with FIONA SAMPSON

Hespere panta fereis hosa fainolis eskedas auos
fereis oin fereis aiga fereis apy materi paida

Evening, you bring back everything the bright dawn scattered:
bring back the ewe, bring back the kid, bring the child back to its mother.

SAPPHO

Ehatähte, hella tähte,
see viib värvud välla pealta,
aub haned aruninasta,
vanad vaipa ju vautab,
noored nurka uinutelleb.
Koidutähte, kurja tähte,
see viib värvud välla peale,
vanad vaibast erutab,
noored nurgast kergitelleb.

Evening star, tender star,
takes the little birds from the field,
takes the geese from the meadow,
puts the old under a blanket,
the young to sleep in the corner.
Morning star, cruel star,
chases the little birds to the field,
gets the old out of bed
raises the young from the corner.

ESTONIAN FOLK SONG

The snow's melting. Water's dripping.
The wind's blowing, gently.
Boughs sway. There's a fire in the stove.
The radiators are warm.
Anu is doing exercises on the piano.
Ott and Tambet are making a snowman.
Maarja's preparing lunch.
The wooden horse is looking in at the window.
I am looking out of the window.
I am writing a poem.
I'm writing that today is Sunday.
That the snow's melting. That water's dripping.
That the wind's blowing, *et cetera*, *et cetera*.

*

*Zwei Dinge erfüllen das Gemüt mit immer neuer und
zunehmender Bewunderung und Ehrfurcht, je öfter und
anhaltender sich das Nachdenken damit beschäftigt: der
gestirnte Himmel über, und das moralische Gesetz in mir.* *

KANT

Through the cellar ceiling
I hear the shouts of children,
their feet trampling, sometimes
a building block falling and sometimes
their mother's nagging voice.
Above these voices there are
more ceilings,
the roof with chimneys and aerials,
and heaven actually begins
here at this very place
beside us, around us
and reaches up to those
awe-inspiring stars.
We too are heaven-dwellers,
the contemplative philosopher
as well as a child throwing its wood blocks onto the floor
and the writer who doesn't know
whether he feels more awe
for the stars in heaven, castles built of wood blocks,
or the heavenly sandstone
outside the cellar walls and below its floor.

*

* 'Two things fill the spirit with renewed and ever greater admiration
and awe the more often and the more sustainedly we reflect upon them.
They are: the starry sky above me and the moral law within me.'

– KANT (*trs. David Constantine*)

White paper and time: I'm filling one,
the other fills itself.
Both so similar. In front of both
I am shy and full of awe.
The poem is like a sheep
in a dark shed with a high threshold.
I feel uneasy when I approach it.
Sight stays outside. Here you can move
only with the help of your hands.
White paper. White wool. In the dark
both simply something not dark. Time
both invisible and visible
as it is outside in broad daylight
where you left your eyesight.
Time: a white wet towel. Poetry trickling out
when you twist it.
The towel drying on a warm pipe
in a dark bathroom.

*

For many years, always in March,
I've felt sorry for these quiet
days and cloudy skies. The arrival
of the real spring has something
frightening in it. Everything
is suddenly new and strange: the doormat, unwashed windows,
willow buds, tufts of grass sticking up through the snow,
the starlings and the moon above the floodplain.
Everything is like a call, everything's tempting and luring you
out of the room, out of home, out of yourself, out of mind;
to flow over land and water, to go somewhere else,
to be somewhere else, somebody else;
and if you cannot then at least
to shout, to dance, to write,
to sing stupid spring songs
in order to soothe this urge.
I can't understand whether it's in the blood or the mind
or somewhere else. Maybe it's the cellular memory
of my ancestors – fish, birds or peasants –
the memory of previous lives awakening in me
an urge to swim to flooded meadows to spawn
to look for a partner and a nesting place
to feel with a hand whether the soil is warm enough;
or something even more mysterious and archaic:
the understanding of a seed that it's time to sprout,
the thrill and fear of yet another death and birth.

*

It's easy to say what's become of the snow
where we went skiing only two weeks ago,
upstream, past the ruins of Jänese tavern and the railway bridge
where on both sides
there's only forest: alder and birch
slanting towards the water, earthworks on both banks
probably left by dredging.
I could say: the snow's gone, melted, flowed
into Peipsi lake and further away, evaporated, soaked into soil.
But I still think of those ski tracks,
of our traces on the snowy river ice...
What have they become? Do such traces
vanish completely, without leaving any traces? And are we
like that snow or those ski tracks?
Or like neither of them? Something different, something else?

*

I was coming from Tähtvere. It was Sunday evening.
I was the only fare to the final stop.
I stepped out. The road was silent: not a single car.
The wind had fallen silent. Only the stars
and the sickle of the new moon shone above the river.
I felt sorry I had to keep going. I'd have liked to step
off the path onto the wasteland and to stop
to look at that moon, those constellations – several of which
I'd forgotten again during the winter – but most of all
at the sky itself, the blue of the sky that was nearly
as deep and strange as once long ago,
twenty years ago, when we sat and drank wine
around a campfire in the nearby forest, and I came
back to Tartu on a village road with a girl,
arms around each other's necks.
The blue is much easier to remember
than names, titles or faces,
even the faces of those you once loved.

*

Once again I think about what I've read: that light and darkness,
good and evil, truth and lies, are mixed up in this world. Certainly
for those who thought like that the world really was alive: everything
was black or white, God's or the Devil's own.
But what will remain of this world split into two camps
if everything becomes infinitely divisible, crumbles
into a whirlwind of particles, flickering of fields?
Will every particle contain some dark and light,
will the opposites be there even in the tiniest of them,
even in zero itself, splitting what is closer and closer
to non-existence? Will the strange
replace the horrible? Will it be easier
to exist?

*

I don't feel at home in this synthetic world
where the good old varnish smell is replaced
by the whiff of acrylic and glyphtal paints
I find it hard, sometimes impossible, to get accustomed to;
where shelves and tables are made of sawdust
and you can play the *Ode to Joy* on a plastic flute
or listen to it in a recording
by some long-dead conductor. Your environment
consists of dead things, people and voices. Life withdraws
in front of us, until there's only wilderness to retreat to.
Or it survives in hideouts beside us:
in flower-pot, aquarium, wall crack, dustbin.
A student awake late at night
puts the book aside and kills some bedbugs
which, as always, leave their holes at a certain hour
and creep into the bed.

*

Spring has indeed come: the willows are in blossom and queen
        bumblebees
are looking for nesting places; fruit flies circle
over the bowl of sour milk; on the kitchen curtain
a big moth's sleeping exactly on a red spot.
A mosquito flies into the cellar room and buzzes around my head.
For some time, sitting at the desk, I've been hearing
a strange noise from a plastic sachet hanging on the wall.
Finally I take it down and have a look: a spider
has fallen into it and is making desperate attempts to get out.

*

The morning began with sunshine – we brought the rugs out
to be aired, sent the children to the sand pit
and ourselves went to the garden where
the dandelions and couch grass were already rampant, the
        strawberry bed
full of flowering corn mint buzzing with bumblebees.
We had to clear everything up, dig the whole patch,
tear out couch grass, horsetail and bindweed root by root.
It took a lot of time. Surely later on
it will be nice to think that we've gone through every bit of soil
with our fingers. In the early afternoon
it was so hot that I even took my shirt off, digging. In the west
clouds were gathering already, and in late afternoon,
when the first beds were ready, it began to rain.
I sowed carrots and turnips
when it was already raining, with my black waterproof on.
At night, before falling asleep, I saw
only earth and roots, roots, roots.

        *

154

I could say: I got out of the bus,
stepping onto the dusty verge where
a young maple and a wild rose grow.
In reality, I jumped into silence
and there was no ground to step on.
The silence closed over my head like water:
I barely noticed the bus leaving
and as I sank deeper and deeper
I heard only my own heartbeats,
seeing the way home glide past
in its own rhythm: lilies of the valley sprouting,
wood sorrel already nearly in blossom,
the anthill covered as if by a brownish quivering veil –
the ants themselves. The Big Pine. The Big Spruce.
Drying hurdles. Sand pit. Traces of a fire.
White birch trunks. The Big Boulder.
And many memories. Silence, the inland sea,
nameless background of all these names,
of all our names.

*

Running for milk I saw wood sorrel in bloom
to the left of the path, and my mind became restless,
feeling its helplessness in front of something primeval and strange
that occasionally – but furtively, evasively –
touches you. In a forest in spring
I feel like a prisoner who has nothing more
than the walls of his cell, scribbled full of words and names,
and memories of free space, landscapes, women
and thirst for all of them. What is there
between me and the forest, between me and the world?
Where is the wall that keeps me apart
from what everything in me thirsts for, the wall
that separates me from this wood sorrel,
these horsetails, cow wheat, wintergreens, from this sprouting
that I must always walk past, that I can never
really touch...? But still – this time
a new thought woke in my besieged mind –
maybe all the time I've sought and longed for
a reality behind this reality; trying to get closer
I've gone further away. For the first time
I understood that transparency itself is nothing less
than what you see through it: the evening sun
shining through petals of wood sorrel.

*

I write a poem every day,
although I'm not quite sure if these texts
should be called poems at all.
It's not difficult, especially now
when it's spring in Tartu, and everything is changing its form:
parks, lawns, branches, buds and clouds
above the town, even the sky and stars.
If only I had enough eyes, ears and time
for this beauty that sucks us in like a whirlpool
covering everything with a poetic veil of hopes
where only one thing sticks out unnaturally:
the half-witted man sitting at the bus stop
taking boots from his dirty maimed feet,
his stick and his woollen cap lying beside him;
the same cap that was on his head
when you saw him that day standing
at the same stop at three in the morning
as the taxi drove you past him and the driver
said, 'That idiot's got hold of some booze again.'

*

We walked the road to Kvissental,
blooming bird cherries on both sides
white clouds of blossom in the midst of a willow thicket.
I broke off a twig of blossom for my son
and showed him the willows: one had vivid green,
the other greyish leaves. 'But why do the willows exist?'
he asked, and it was difficult to find an answer.
I told him the trees simply exist without knowing
or thinking anything. He probably didn't understand
my idea. But how can I speak
for trees? We reached the river.
We went to the old jetty that was swaying
in waves from passing motor boats;
we sat on an old beam, seeing how glittering blue
this river was, which in the north passes through forest;
seeing how dandelions, buttercups and ash
were germinating in the dirt between the pier planks.
We caught some caddis worms and put them back in the river;
we washed our sweaty and dusty faces
in the greenish flowing water, and began our trip back home.

*

My aunt knew them well. I know
only their names and what other people have told me:
tinkers, haberdashers, attorneys, doctors,
Genss, Michelson, Itzkowitsch, Gulkowitsch...
Where are they now? Some of them were lucky enough
to be buried in this cemetery under a slab with Hebrew lettering.
But those my aunt met on the streets of German-occupied Tartu,
with a yellow star sewn to their clothes, and to whom
she even dared to speak to the horror of her friends:
they are not here, they are scattered
into nameless graves, ditches and pits
in many places, many countries, homeless in death
as in life. Maybe some of them are hovering
in the air as particles of ash, and have not yet
descended to earth. I've thought
that if I were a physicist I would like to study dust,
everything that's hovering in the air, dancing in sunlight,
getting into eyes and mouths, into the ice of Greenland
or between the books on the shelf. Maybe one day
I would have met you,
Isaac, Mordechai, Sarah, Esther, Sulamith
and whoever you were. Maybe even today I breathed in
something of you with this intoxicating spring air;
maybe a flake of you fell today on the white white
apple blossom in my grandfather's garden
or on my grey hair.

*

The sky's overcast. The warm wind creeps under your shirt.
A spotted cat walks slowly towards the dusk.
Dusk moves slowly towards the spotted cat.
A neighbour's wife is taking clothes from the line.
I don't see her, I only see the clothes vanishing
one by one. I see the white lilac.
Narcissi and carnations. And lights
shining far away on the other side of the river. One recorder.
One radio. One reed warbler. And many,
many nightingales.

*

Silence is always here and everywhere;
sometimes we simply hear it more clearly:
fog covers the meadow, the barn door is open,
a redwing's singing over there, a white
moth circles incessantly around the elm branch
and the branch itself is still swaying imperceptibly
against the background of the evening sky.
The dusk robs us all of faces and names,
only the difference between light and dark remains.
The heart of a midsummer's night:
the old watch on the desk
is suddenly ticking so terribly loudly.

*

This other life only begins in the evening
when the wind dies down, the clouds
gather on the horizon waiting for tomorrow
and the aroma of honeysuckle is flooding
courtyard and garden.
The heron alights at the pond and stays still
waiting. Through the bird cherries
I see something light close to the water,
and somehow it is hard to believe it's anything other
than just a spot of bright evening sky
reflected on the still surface whose peace
is disturbed only by some water insect
or a line drawn by the dorsal fin
of a carp.

*

I don't want to write courtly poetry any more,
the poetry of a horseman who sees the world only
from the eyeholes of my helmet
and in whose mind and language the horse-trot has left
its indelible *tata-rata*, *tata-rata*,
and who's always racing over and past everything.
In my life and poetry I've always wanted
to be a pedestrian, a wandering scholar who can
sit down on every hillside that's to his liking,
look at everything he wants to,
look at the bumblebee who searches
each blossom of the red clover in turn
and then follow it with his eyes until it vanishes
in the blue of the summer sky; to stay for a while
without thinking, just like that,
enjoying all this transient beauty
until the cool shadow of a cloud
falls upon me, reminding me
that it's time to stand up and go: evening
is approaching, I must find accommodation somewhere
and tomorrow at daybreak start again, to reach
the town before the gates close.
Maybe I'll find some work there
writing letters, composing verse
and teaching Latin to boys (and even girls)
of the better families.

However, a reminiscence of this hillside, this bumblebee
and this shadow of a cloud will remain, and will sometimes
sound in the background of my songs about summer,
about birds singing and, of course, about Venus
and some buxom tavern-maid who was ready
to share with a poor scholar, free, just for a song he made,
what they call love. Yes

in one of my songs I spoke of the bumblebee
on the red clover-blossom and of the cool shadow
of the cloud on the face of the wanderer
who suddenly thought he didn't know
how to write about it all in Latin... And now,
seven hundred years later, all I remember
are these lines:

Qualis in aestivo sudo
nova, mira pulchritudo
subito in omnibus

rebus, avibus, insectis;
novis, laetis et perfectis
patet mundus sensibus.

*

Only at dusk do eyes really begin to see.
The colours of flowers become lucid and bright
before night extinguishes them: carnations, yellow roses,
meadow-vetch and buttercups.
The wind has died down and the sky
– the faded, nearly invisible
background of all our comings and goings –
is suddenly here, just above the treetops and pylons,
shining through foliage and above the roof of the house
in all its depth and blueness. Behind the outhouse
Venus appears; to the right of the pole of the well, Jupiter:
once two gods, now two stars.

*

A last cloud moves across the sky from west to east.
A last bee alights on the flight board of the hive.
A last bird flies over the garden into the spruce hedge.
I see only its hurrying silhouette
against the background of the sky, and a swaying branch
there where it vanished. Has it a nest there?
The voice of the corncrake comes nearer and nearer.
Now it's just behind the fence. Another crake
answers it from the roadside field. Maybe
they will meet one another tonight. Maybe tomorrow night.

*

The rain stops and, for an instant, the sun emerges from clouds.
The shadow of the pen appears on the white paper.
A redwing is singing somewhere. The wind rises
and raindrops roll off the leaves of the honeysuckle.
They say I haven't written as suggestively as in my youth,
in the book *Of dust and colours*. The sun
casts a yellowish light on the quivering green world
and vanishes once again behind a cloud. I remember
that I must make a roof for the empty beehive
where the wasps nested. In the autumn I must trim down
some apple tree branches growing in front of the loft door
that are a nuisance when we want to put hay in the loft. Also
I should wash some used preserve cans:
they're good for nails or to mix paint.
When I tried for the first time seriously to write a poem,
it was in Russian. It begins like this:

Nad...i mrachnym Baikalom
odinokaya chayka letit...

Isn't it suggestive?
There is a time for everything. At the gate
the water ash, *Ptelea trifoliata*, is in bloom
and the rye stalks are already rustling dry.

*

There are so many insects this summer.
As soon as you go into the garden
a buzzing swarm of flies besieges you.
The bumblebees are nesting in boxes you made for birds,
the wasps have made their nests in hazel bushes.
And sitting at your desk in the attic room
you constantly hear a buzzing, and don't know
whether it's the sound of bumblebees, wasps,
electric wires,
a plane in the skies, a car on the road,
or the voice of life itself wanting to tell you something
from the inside, from your inner self.

*

There are as many worlds as grains of sand on a beach.
Big and small, round and square,
light and dark, age-old and transient:
some stand still, some go round,
some are alone, some in swarms;
and in every one of these big and small,
round and square, light and dark,
age-old and transient worlds there are seas and beaches,
and plenty of sand on those beaches;
and in each grain of sand there are as many worlds
as grains of sand on a beach, big and small,
round and square. In some of them
Buddha is already born, on some of them
he's not yet born, in some of them
he is living and teaching just now.
In one of them I'm sitting at my desk in the attic room
and a wood warbler, *Phylloscopus sibilatrix*,
flies up to my window, so I can see close up
the yellow stripe above its dark eye
and how it knocks with its beak
on the window-pane and then flies away.

*

It makes little sense to talk about the subconscious,
maybe even about consciousness itself:
there are no borders, no ground, there's nothing
to stand on. I have a mind and a face,
but the mind and face have no me.
Everything reaches everything: it's at once
both conscious, subconscious and unconscious
and everything else. But what, then,
is all that stuff with so many names: anger, pain,
anxiety, sadness? Even being angry, being in pain:
I can't believe they really exist.
What could we compare them to in this floating world?
With the wind coming and going, with waves;
with cracks, an invisible line without breath
running though this beautiful midsummer evening.
If everything is in everything then maybe
in this everything are even the things
that separate everything from everything:
cracks, lines, borders... barbed wire
on which every spring a whinchat sings
and where tufts of goats' or lambs' wool flutter in the breeze.

*

There is no God,
there is no director,
there is no conductor.
The world makes itself happen,
the play plays itself,
the orchestra plays itself.
And if the violin drops from somebody's hand
and their heart stops beating
the man and his death never meet:
there's nothing behind the glass;
the other side is nothing, is just a mirror
where my own fear regards me
with big eyes.
And behind this fear,
if only you look carefully enough,
there are grass and sunflowers
turning slowly by themselves towards the sun
without a God, a director, a conductor.

*

The world doesn't consist of matter or spirit,
of fields, particles or dynamic geometry.
The world consists of questions and answers,
the world is *wen-do* or *kong-an*
(in Japanese *mondo* and *koan*). Today at noon
a relative of mine drove up in his jeep
and told me that next Thursday I have to go to a funeral:
V.'s twelve-year-old son fell
from the stable-loft onto a concrete floor
and died two days later without regaining consciousness.
I know this too is a question.
I know there's an answer here. I know
I should know the answer but...

*

Late summer: a faded old watercolour
more and more lacking in colour and depth.
As every autumn, big clumsy flies
creep through cracks into rooms
and can't find the way out. In the evening clouds gather
in the sky but there's not even a dew at night. Jays
pick the last peas from the bed.
Flocks of thrushes light on rowan trees.
We've seen it so many times already. The long drought
has left its imprint on our faces and thoughts.
And it's hard to believe there's anything new
under the sun, except the wind and some delusory clouds,
meteor-flashes in the night sky and other
accidental things that you for some reason
take notice of and keep in mind, like the earwig
that turned around and around on the gravel path
beside our house.

*

The full moon south-east above Piigaste forest.
A ripe apple falling with a thump
from the crab-apple tree behind the privy.
Two round things calling to my mind
Chinese poetry and the round teaching
of hua-yen philosophy: every single thing
contains all other things,
as I have several times thought and said,
and cannot but think and say once again,
tonight, some nights before the autumn equinox.

*

I told the students about the beginning of Greek culture.
Telling them the Hittite story of Ullikummi I said
that among known Lydian inscriptions there are some
poetic texts, but they can hardly be read. I also talked about Homer
and his gods, about the tomb of Zeus on Crete
and the religion of Mithra which proclaims
that the world is a battleground of two mighty adversaries –
the forces of Good and Evil, Truth and Lie, Dark and Light –
and the faithful are Mithra's soldiers, the soldiers of Light
in this age-old war where stone stands against stone,
tree against tree, animal against animal, man against man.
Then I finished and took the bus home.
I was tired and had a terrible thirst.

*

From stalks and curls of pine-bark
the flycatcher builds its nest.
From gravel and pebbles
the glaciers have built hills and drumlins.
From short poems
I put together my own China:
it's so easy to walk and breathe
in your company,
Tao Yuanming, Li Bo, Meng Haoran.

*

from

SUMMERS AND SPRINGS

(1995/2004)

translated by
JAAN KAPLINSKI
with FIONA SAMPSON

In the morning I was presented to President Mitterrand,
in the evening I weeded-out nettles under the currant bushes.
A lot happened in between; the ride from Tallinn to Tartu and to
        our country home
through the spring we had waited so long for,
and that came, as always, unexpectedly,
all at once changing serious greyish Estonia
into a primary school child's drawing in pale green,
into a play-landscape where mayflies, mayors and cars
are all somewhat tiny and ridiculous... In the evening
I saw the full moon rise above the alder grove. Two bats
circled over the courtyard. The President's hand
was soft and warm. As were his eyes
where fatigue was, in a curious way,
mingled with force, and depth with banality.
He had bottomless night eyes
with something mysterious in them
like the paths of moles underground
or the places where bats hibernate and sleep.

*

The radio's talking about the Tiananmen bloodbath.
It was three years ago. Just before that
I was there too: the square was empty, the sun shining.
At night it was freezing, but the city air
was full of dust. I don't know whether it came
from the Gobi desert or from building sites
in the city itself. At the other end of the square
huge cauldrons were boiling: a bowl of rice
with sauce and salad for less than a dollar.
I still remember its taste
as I remember young men whispering
in all the cities at the doors of all the hotels:
exchange money exchange money exchange change.

*

The sea doesn't want to make waves.
The wind doesn't want to blow.
Everything wants balance, peace
and seeking peace has no peace.
If you understand this, does it
change something? Can you be peaceful
even where there is no peace?
Is it a different kind of peace?
Questions all over again. Answers
are few, as always.
The wave goes up and down.
A flock of birds flies low to NNE.
This, too, is a wave. Thought is waves, too.

*

God has left us: I felt this clearly
loosening the earth around a rhubarb plant.
It was black and moist. I don't know where he is,
only a shelf full of sacred books remains of him,
a couple of wax candles, a prayer wheel and a little bell.
Coming back to the house I thought
there might still be something: the smell of lilac and honeysuckle.
Then suddenly I imagined a child's face
there, on the other side, in eternity
looking here, into time, regarding wide-eyed
our comings, goings and doings in this time-aquarium
under the light of the sun going down;
and falling asleep under a water-lily leaf
somewhere far away in the west.

*

The possibility of rain... If rain is possible
everything is possible: spinach, lettuce, radish and dill,
even carrots and potatoes, even black
and red currants, even swallows
above the pond where you can see
the reflection of the full moon, and bats flying.
The children finish playing badminton and go in.
There's a haze to the west. Little by little
the fatigue in my limbs changes to optimism. I dream
I borrow a plane to fly to Cologne.
I must go in too. The sky's nearly dark,
a half-moon shining through birch branches.
Suddenly I feel myself like an alchemist's retort
where all this – heat, boredom,
hope and new thoughts –
is melting into something strange, colourful and new.

*

A fit body doesn't exist. There are only space,
extension, endless possibilities,
the fact that you can touch that birch tree there,
fetch the big white stone from the ditch.
The sick body is everywhere: the room, courtyard,
path to the well, the house and the pale-blue sky
are all full of it. The sick body
is so big that everything touches,
hurts and injures it. A spruce branch swaying
at the fence comes in and bruises your face.
The wind swinging the witches' broom
blows through your breast.
The swallows' cries hit you like hammer blows.
Night falls like an old wet blanket on your eyes and mouth.

*

The age-old dream of mankind: to fly like a bird. A fairy tale come true not as a fairy tale but as a machine, an airline company that puts in motion lots of other machines: wheels, axes, levers and drives that sell you a ticket, ask SMOKING – NON-SMOKING, put you in a pigeonhole – BUSINESS CLASS, TOURIST CLASS, EUROCLASS, ECONOMY CLASS – and pack you into a huge cigar box in A, B, D, E or F, give you dinner, offer you cigarettes, earrings, watches, perfume and sweets. In business class drinks are free, elsewhere only the smiles and the air are free, but during the flight the air becomes denser and denser and you feel more and more of an urge to jump out, to break out of this cigar box, in order to really fly or at least fall into these white shining clouds, through which you can't see whether there is sea or land under you and on whose far edge another plane is creeping toward Frankfurt like a cockroach on a white wool blanket.

*

One day you will do everything for the last time: breathe, make love, drink, sleep and wake up. Maybe even think. One day you will visit Paris for the last time. If you knew when, you'd go somewhere you felt suited you. No, not to the Louvre, not to the Pantheon, not to a street café, not to a library, but to the botanical gardens, to the Jardin des Plantes where you have a chance to encounter the dandelion, wood sorrel and mallow who will acknowledge you. As you will be acknowledged by the silence that took you by the hand, helping you to overcome fear in your home on University Street in Tartu late one afternoon when everyone else was away. You were sitting on the sofa with a book in your hand. Darkness was falling. Distant voices changed their tone and the shadows crept out from under the wardrobes and beds. It's the same silence that was waiting for you in an old outhouse full of old wooden vessels and dust that nobody had cleaned up for years. The silence that took hold of you like a voiceless dark vortex dragging you into depths whose bottom you haven't yet reached. If there is any bottom at all: maybe there is only the echo, a rumble that has come nearer with every year, the deafening, dizzying TE DEUM or OM MANI PADME HUM of free fall, of freedom.

*

Evening's coming. The land and the forest meet
the big cool silence that is disturbed
only by the buzz of gnats and the warning cry of a nightingale
from the bushes near our sauna. I come back from the garden
through chill alternating with warmth: it reminds me
of summers in childhood when I cycled
through similar waves of cold and warmth,
through the smell of pine trees and strawberries. Childhood.
No, I'd never like to get it back.
There was a shadow lying on my childhood. I have always
fled this shadow, am fleeing it even now,
although I feel that when I'm finally out of its reach
there will be only a void, a cool voiceless void
with pine bark peelings, feathers and ourselves
caught in a dizzying vortex, a free fall
from night to morning, from morning to night.

*

It's raining again, and Estonia is cooling like a sauna, like a fireplace. The rain is cold. Big drops fall from the balcony onto the window box that stayed empty this summer. Grandmother was too weak to grow flowers in the box as she had done every year, and she complained more and more. This summer she spent a couple of weeks in the countryside at her cousin's, she even wrote us a letter from there, but then we got a message that she had fallen very ill. She was taken to the hospital in town, and they found she had a large intestinal cancer. She never recovered from surgery but lived some days in a high fever, in a mental twilight, speaking in a loud voice to her dead relatives as if they'd come to take her. Maybe they really had, maybe she saw something we couldn't see. But we could never ask her about that.

*

The centre of the world is here, in Manchester.
I carry it with me
as we all do. The centre of the world
pierces me, the way a pin
pierces the body of an insect.
The centre of the world
is the pain.

*

My poems often aren't poems; they're parts of a long declaration of love to the world, a long poetic list of people and things I love. When I was young I was fond of my thoughts, my feelings, my longing and joy. I approached the world like a hot air balloon which covered everything up. With the years the balloon has cooled down, shrunk, and I see more and more of other things, I see simply what is. This *simply what is* has always seemed odd to me. Sometimes I experience this oddity as elevated, sometimes it's simply funny. The feeling of oddity has never disappeared. It's probably deeper and more self-conscious than ever.

The wall clock was made in Valga in 1902, and it's still going quite well. It could even strike, if I had a chain for the other weight. But I don't believe I could get accustomed to a wall clock that struck hours. Now it's showing 11. It's December 31st, 1992. As often before, I am writing something in the last hour of the year. I'm not sure I would like to call it a poem. It's not taking much time, and the emotional atmosphere of the last hour of the year suits writing well. The tick-tock of the old clock suits this atmosphere well too. I think that maybe the dead clockmaker from Valga is sending his greetings to me and my family this way. I can't do the same to him.

*

Less and less space for flying. I don't know whether my wings have grown longer or the walls and ceiling of this room have shrunk, so that my left wing nearly touches the wall to my left and my right wing the wall to my right. When I rise a little my head touches the ceiling and my hair get chalky. It's good that I have grey hair, otherwise a glance at my head would show how little space I have left. At the moment you can probably only see it from my eyes, but it's not our custom to look into the eyes of other people, especially on New Year's Eve when all the cats and all eyes are grey in the same way.

*

More and more empty words, the tricolour under grey clouds, music, new ways of saying and doing things. You bow, smile, thank, ask questions, vote. But deep inside you a little child's voice is shouting louder and louder: 'How did I get here?'

Is this your home or a place of punishment, an alien bleak piece of land set against an alien bleak sea, an alien language and alien people to whom you must return again and again from dreams where you could be on these islands or in China, in Greece, in the West Coast cedar forests? We bow, we smile, we thank, we ask questions. The phone rings, you're caught by the phone line like a fish by a hook. Was it you somebody wanted to catch or are you just bait for somebody bigger and more important who lives here, on this bleak land in this bleak sea, and who is lured out of the depths by your story, your poem or simply by your despair?

*

I saw something white far away at the roadside. At first I took it for a bike, then I realised that it was just a bunch of white *umbelliferae*. All morning I'd tried to read a poem by Ruan Ji, but with little success. There were too many words there meaning sadness, sorrow, pain and trouble. It seems there are dozens of such words in Chinese: this certainly means that the Chinese had a sophisticated culture of mourning and grieving. Early in the day the sun was shining, then grey clouds began rising from the north and it got chilly, with drizzle from time to time. I felt nearly as sad as the Chinese poet who lived 1,700 years ago. But I know from my own experience that a certain kind of sadness is connected with the birth or rebirth of your poetic gift. It's painful: poems aren't born easily, they always break something in you, rip you apart, take away a piece of your flesh, leaving a scar like those you got falling off your bike on a stony road or cutting your finger with a knife.

*

The weather changed overnight. The clouds that were like grey wolves changed into white sheep, creeping innocently up from behind the spruce hedge that leads to the neighbour's oat field. The granary roof which had turned nearly black with rain dried out and became light grey again. I wanted to do nothing but simply to be and to walk around in the midst of this summer which had finally arrived. We always feel it's too short, we have too little of it. Everything is suddenly clearer, is open, turned outwards, towards others, towards the clouds, towards light. I stood on the jetty, closed my eyes and listened to the voices of summer: the forest was murmuring, aspen leaves were rustling, and a late finch was singing in the alder grove. A school of tiny carp swam in the pond and a frog was quacking on the bank. I thought that I would like to be like these frogs: I would lie half the day in water and croak now and then. But one thought wouldn't let me go. A summer thought, a summer poem, was striving, was climbing higher and higher, believing that it would soon reach a surface, a wall. A thought that summer is like a huge glass bell around us and above us, catching all our voices and giving them a clearer sound.

Summer is a piece of our phylogenetic childhood that we carry with us as a deep dim memory. We don't go back to Africa where we come from, as swallows and storks do. But once a year Africa comes here, meets us here. Summer comes to us like a great psychoanalyst, a phylogenetic Freud. It's like a great wizard, it makes wonderful things: teaches fledglings to fly, transforms newts into real frogs and the meadow into a huge flowerbed. On some still, worm mornings it can even transform us into something more human. I dare not say whether it means we become more ourselves. But on a mild summer evening it means a great deal.

*

193

My eyesight's weakening. I don't see the plants in the lawn beneath my feet as sharply as before. And I always have the feeling that I haven't seen them enough. I would like to look, to see them with more reality, more in-depth; to look this patch of lawn, these knot-grasses, this clover, these *Alchemillas*, these *Plantagos*, these dandelions into myself. Or to look myself into them, to be for a while a stem of grass, a winding stem of vetch, a white clover blossom bending under the weight of a black bumblebee. I think I am simply afraid. I'm afraid that I still don't see all this with enough reality, so that I could take a patch of the lawn with me into the time when my eyes will see no more. In fact, I would like to take something of all this Over There, to the other side. I am afraid that, once there, I will have little left other than words: sentences and thoughts but no leaves of grass, no patch of lawn with dead oak leaves from last summer, no bumble bee in flight and no chirping of grasshoppers announcing midsummer.

I have gone through this world like a tourist through a museum. I've tried to glean something from these thousands of displays, to keep something essential in mind. But after visiting time is over, when the warden says that the museum is closing, there will be hopelessly little that I can remember. And lying there in an empty hotel room I'll think that during my whole life I have been unhappily in love with this wonderful world we have to hurry through. It's because of this unhappy love I want to get something of my own, to buy something really belonging to myself, as a man unable to win the love of a woman tries to turn her into his possession. But he too will finally have only an empty room and a memory where the words, sentences and thoughts have eaten up, forced out all the clover blossoms, Althaea leaves and the chirping of the first grasshoppers, where his eyes cannot recall the flowering of white clover or that curve of female hips he hoped was a gateway to another, more real world.

*

194

The world is a single event.
Events have no beginning and no end.
The wind moves the oak leaves,
the oak leaves move in the wind.
In fact there's no border
between the oak leaves and the wind,
no difference between the wind and the leaves and twigs
it moves, between the wind and this windy day
where the weather's changing, and for an instant
you understand the oneness of the leaves and the wind,
and a little green beetle
tumbles from the oak into your hair.

*

I opened the Russian-Chinese dictionary:
there between two pages was a tiny insect.
It spread its wings and flew away.
I lost sight of it, maybe
it's still struggling on the window pane
or has died there like so many insects or succeeded
in getting out into the open. Like some of us.
For a while I wondered if it couldn't have been
a word, a sign from the dictionary
which had had enough and wanted to become
something else, something more than a sign,
a hieroglyph under the cold glass covers
of this world, of this life.

*

I've thought that I thought about death, but in fact I don't know how one should think of death. Death is probably very hard, as hard as life, but life is something you live piece by piece, whereas you die once and for all... Once and for all you have to tear away all the lived life – seven, seventeen, seventy, and if someone is very strong, eighty years – and to let them fall into an abyss, into the void. A tiny pale bodiless soulless somebody lingers for moment on the rim of the abyss. This is the one who has thrown away his life; it would be better to say he has let it loose. Seen from the other side life is death, life and death are one and the same thing. Life is something you must keep and guard all the time like a rat in a cage. Because it is so hard to think of death, I prefer to think of the currants: black, red and white currants which are so ripe that they fall when you touch the bush.

*

I don't have a land or a sky of my own.
I only have a little white cloud
which I met once, as a schoolboy
lying in the courtyard on a pile of twigs
looking into the sky. There were martins
and clouds: this one, my only one, too.
I would recognise it today too,
through all the transformations,
if only I had time just to lie there
idly on a pile of twigs in the courtyard.

*

THE SOUL RETURNING

(1973-75)

translated by
JAAN KAPLINSKI
with FIONA SAMPSON

The Soul Returning

Never
wanted
that

never
wanted
to be
I
me

everything
by
chance

poem
called
a poem

pain
called
something
else

coming
going
by
itself

names
always
a trouble

always stumbling
at words
at me
at names
at the nameless

in reality there is no MUST
there is
nothing you must begin or end

no must
no need to
exist
no needs before
you exist
need something

o
little flames
in empty space
little islands in the empty ocean
air
water
clouds
song
have more understanding
than I have

be more
than I am

but somewhere and with something you must begin

words
have more understanding
than you have

be open
stay open
earth air
islands
spaces

here is the beginning
here
it has begun

here

and everywhere
a beginning
an end
begun
together

a beginning
an end
in roots
as well as leaves
in stamina
as well as pistils

leaves
treetops

in reality everything is falling we all are falling that is the same as
turning around coming and going being and not being and
because of that the most stupid questions are where from for what
a purpose why for whose sake

in reality I have never wanted to speak to write poems about
anything other than free fall freedom but if I want to look out
there is something a snowstorm or a huge white bird taking flight
I cannot say where from or where to if I want to look I am small
and silly and there is a cold pane between me and the darkness
and I cannot even shout into that night of snow and birds into
that white birdfeather-darkness the only word that would explain
everything be the beginning of everything

I know I am small and silly I am old and tired I was a poet I was
I but in reality there was no me there was only this word this
dreadful white word I have bent down to see through this evening
this everlasting snowstorm to look through myself throught the
dark windowpane and dark space through it all through myself
and through my non-existence

202

but there is
no answer
because
there was
no question

the owl flies up
cranes are
flying overhead
I lie
under the alder trees
in tears

sacred
earth
sacred heaven

now
suddenly
forever

a little flame
two eyes
taking wing
from the granary roof
from the ship mast

what what
are you full of
night of
snowstorm

in reality I had to write something else this something else was
nearly ready but there was no beginning no beginning and no title

titles are not important but beginning how can something be
without a beginning although I do not name it do not call it a
poem a cycle of poems an elegy an incantation a spell a piece of
shamanism a bullshit modern poem but beginning a beginning is

here
I am now
here
in the

beginning

from beginning
to end
always

in reality tomorrow I should go to Tallinn to the capital to a
meeting of the Writers' Union where they will discuss problems
of poetry my wife and mother-in-law ask me if I can stay at home
if I can just not go whether there will be worries what people in
the Writers' union will think of me and what they should say if
there is a call from the Writers' Union

in reality everything is much simpler I simply do not exist have
not existed for a long time already Jaan Kaplinski or whatever was
his name was came drove through the snowy forest stopped to
listen to the snowstorm and everything changed into birds and
poems he himself too

he
himself
too

let the poems themselves have a meeting let them discuss poets'
problems they know better they make somebody a poet they come
if they will as they will when they will there is nothing else we
should discuss at a poets' meeting but the poems will never tell
you that

a word comes throu
gh the windy ni
ght and cuts yo
u in two

in reality stupidity is as strange as wisdom but I am rarely able to
understand it

I would like to understand stupidity

I would like to be absent from writers' meetings

if I would like anything at all I
would like
to listen
to hear
to come
through
the
forest
to bow
into the
darkness
and
take
two handfuls of

white
snow

but
I stumble
on myself
as on wet stones
in the Ahja river
of my childhood
but this is
even more
than
the Ahja

I wanted to write something that would be the same as what the
shaman sings when the soul somebody's soul is gone is astray and
the shaman must go and look for it somewhere in another world
and bring it back maybe it is possible to call the soul back with a
song with a poem too

in reality I can perhaps say that this dreadful white word behind
the windowpane is the soul resting there in the snowstorm head
covered by the soft white wings of its own non-existence
eyes closed
dreaming of
something

but perhaps you are dreaming yourself and your soul a soul is
longing to see you and to wake you from the other side of that
darkness

a soul
a big
water
coming

from the   come back
beginning   through
                            the life
pure   that wasn't
simple   really
big   a life
confidence   up to the very
that the voice   end of
has reached it   oblivion

everything is different but we can ask where from where to and
why we are just coming going and falling through daytimes and
nighttimes and shadows are falling on us and through us

shadows of fire
shadows of water
shadows of rain
shadows of eclipses
shadows of makeshift animals
on a whitewashed
hospital
wall
shadow theatre
theatre
of
eclipses

I do not know whether they understand it I don't but I feel this
shadow that is more than just a shadow darkness the cold
polished pane of darkness and I am small and silly and always
miss the direction although I am not so stupid as to say it must
be downward or downhill not to speak of life and death

simply
the dog whines
behind the door
the old spinning wheel
falls apart
my two boys
are playing
in the sandbox
with broken
spoons

David Oistrakh
is playing
in a sand...
with a broken violin

but me
for me
how long yet
all this

this voice
that
came back
remaining
as snow
as ice

in reality poetry is not poetry at all even less is it literature
something defined obligatory something that has to be just this
way and not another

in reality there is much more much more than sorrow and joy this
getting lighter getting darker in the forest and in the apple
orchard your playground and that of your children something just
here that remains unknown to you throughout your life

and this bird this bird which I am listening to how can we
summon it through this icy cold darkness

although I know it's not really like that

but I just like being a shadow a flame in this big dark wind

how can we
forget
again and again
these other
landscapes
and rivers
from
who knows where
going
who knows where

although

I have
been there

although
although

I have
met
known them

although

I don't know
whether it means
above
on
in
out

what has
meaning
is only
to reconcile yourself

with these landscapes
people
if you can
find
any

are there
any borders
between
oneself
and something
somebody
else

am I standing
in a sluice-gate
in a furnace-mouth
am I
burning
or flowing

flame
fire-
fall
water-
fall
roaring
all
around

burnt birds
under
another heaven
singing
the same
unfinished

song
drowned fish
laughing
over the
bones
of fishermen

what a joy
that
quenches
love
and hate

in a
furnace mouth
in a
sluice-gate
high up
deep down

everything
burnt
flown
forgotten

hills
like stones
pebbles
or sand
tumbled
drifted
into valleys

clover
growing
on tracks

one single
time-cricket
sawing
on both sides
of the
threshold of
hearing

beyond
the window
snow melting
into
strange
round
drops

you were
away
so long
you were
so long
coming back

what a
corner
of the house
what a
fireplace
a pebble
underfoot
does still
recognise
you

amidst this
echoless

listlessness
if you
yourself
are a part
a particle
of this
listlessness

you
a part
of
it
them
us
all

a voice
is
always
on the
other side
here
deep down

but it
does not
speak
does not
answer

who hasn't
called the
ladybird
by
its name
or an owl

from the night
a flame
from the fire

called home
your
self
your
soul

jaan
little jaan
johnny

come home souls come home
come home souls

but
nobody
speaks
answers

ladybird has
flown
away

time
flown
away
reached
its end

everything
burnt
flown
forgotten

they believed that the ladybird knew the way from one world to another so it could show the way home to one who was lost they believed that the souls of the dead visited the living

in poetry it would be so easy to say that I believe it too but I can't do that because the relationship betwen ladybirds and people between living and dead is much more complicated after all unfortunately this relationship seems not to exist any more we are separated from everybody else free from everybody else from ladybirds other worlds from the dead and living from the soul from our own soul

and it is of little help if I write a poem or something heaven knows what with the title the soul returning if I even put a bowl with gruel in the sauna loft I still have a sauna and the sauna has a loft and it's me who goes out in the darkness and summons the souls calls them back home

but the Estonian people banished their souls banished them and let pastors and priests exorcise them cut down the sacred trees and broke the stones with fire in order to get a strip of land to cultivate what else could he do the poor boor who hoped that now finally he could buy freedom that he could buy himself free with money with hard work with business with cheating with writing with singing with making music with staging plays...

but freedom one can buy and sell has a price its price is a signature and something more something tiny a soul a little soul that lived in a linden tree or a juniper or behind the old oven and ate a bit of everything fresh be it meat milk or new grain it was this same soul that was the price of freedom svoboda freiheit and of course of gratitude prayers songs and songfestivals

Let us praise our Emperor
let us honour Alexander
who has pitied us poor people
who has had Mercy upon the miserable
heard the wailing of the wretched
seen the tears of the dispossessed

but to your souls to your soul you Estonian people said go away
from here go to a place where the foot of man never will step and
the soul answered o how could I who have lived in this tree for
two thousand years have thought that I would have to leave it

when the soul asked you where must I go you said go to the
Ghost Island the soul answered there are so many of us there
already that there is no place even for a needle to stand but
nevertheless you banished it

boor and dandy dandy and boor what is the difference who
remained who has left what is the difference between God and
matter heaven and hell modern and postmodern lower middle and
upper middle Apolla and Dionysus pentecostal and episcopal
conservative and liberal where is the soul nothing has a soul
nobody has a soul

everything is soullless everything without a soul bread and
circuses theatre and movies literature and art ideas and problems
worries and victories spirit and power

in reality everything is so full of emptiness that I cannot understand
how something can exist and last at all how can we live this life
that is no life at all is nothing at all how can everything be as if
nothing else existed as if this emptiness did not exist in us nor
the strange little dot caught in this world-bubble where everything
except us is so new still unborn still to be born where

everything   always
reaches   ready
outside   to die
itself   to be
                    reborn

everything
is   this voice

this word
this
sprouting
spore
of a fern

welcome
welcome
kaplinski
welcome
spores
seeds
water-
drops on
pistils
welcome
body

welcome
mind
me and
you
welcome
light
welcome
winter
welcome
everything
forgotten
unforgettable
today
tomorrow
always

angry thoughts angry words rising to the surface bubbles on black
marsh water must I say welcome to you too comers and goers
decaying body in decaying bed to the truth that the soul is astray
and you cannot find sleep that everyone goes turns around
without a soul breathing air where there is no soul or spirit left
falling little by little swifter and swifter from their sauna loft
sauna bench their house their car with their sauna with their car
with their self through this town through this country through
these streets and avenues angry comers angry goers angry streets
full of angry people and angry cars rising to the surface rising or
falling into an empty wind through clean dark marsh water

are they are we more than these thought bubbles welcome then
welcome and goodbye drink us roots breathe us leaves blow us
away wind blow us into this dance of dust particles that is neither
better nor worse with us or without us and let us never want to
be something else that something else

I don't know
why
I am
there
why
I don't know
I am
there
I don't
know
what
I know
who
what
I am
whether
if
I am
at all
what
pro-

noun
must I
use
when
nothing
remains
nor
is

a
huge
empty
world
always
opening
into huge
eyes
that do
not see
anything
but light

I have never been able I never could say a word without keeping
this in mind however I couldn't not say these words is it to find
some ground under my feet a centre for my world a centre that
does not exist that cannot exist why then do we seek it or do we
seek something else something hidden under a false name in a
false place a fragment of real understanding that would clear away
this cataract between us and the emptimess

we see something but it is not light we see because we do not see
light everything every one of us is a fragment of something I cannot
but call light although I know there is no darkness it cannot reach
there is no darkness but seen from our side everything is just frag-
ments of darkness made of shards of light around us separating us
from everything else and from ourselves words from meanings and

there is no answer to the question why real becomes unreal only
words words words deceptive empty words verbs proverbs adverbs
nouns pronouns going on around us and if there is something
connecting us it is the wind of these wings the words reach some-
where our sight doesn't reach one can put more things together from
words than there is in them or in us the words are the first cutting
through this grey cataract words can sometimes take flight and arrive
somewhere they call us to follow them but we don't go we are looking
for the opening that is not yet closed and when we see what is below
and what is above we are frightened and turn back we cling to every-
thing to a church tower an exclamation mark a spider's web to stop
falling into this reverberating sea of petals into billows suddenly so
near and then everyhting goes off and the words some back tired
and compliant as a poem or a recollection as notes on a scale or
swallows on a wire and only the depth once experienced once seen
remains as a humming an outstretched hand on the bottom of our
memory as a cry for help to accompany us to the very end

empty stupid dear words who always cover my wounds with your
voiceless dappled wings o light light have you spoken to me in my
own tiny flakes of words

world
not yet
awake
to
any dream
any sleep
to any
shadowy stripe
of memory
to despair
this is
our only hope
that somebody
something
comes

cuts
the wrong soul
from the
wrong body
takes
apart
the world
knitted together
in the
wrong way
bringing back
the only
true
soul

life is sad endless watching of the fire putting the fire to bed waking
fire up from evening to evening morning to morning from generation
to generation from an old house into a new house but it is always
older than us we are its we are your children's children old good
sad fire burning is dying and sadness the sadness of a flame in the
black eyes of the world sadness of life itself because of its beginning
and after the end without a beginning and without an end simply
as it is in this wonder that shines from outside into all things that
shines from inside out of all things is there a time is there a name
is there an eye for this sole this most wonderful thing that is

around which
is
still circling
your SELF
bewitched
into
a word
your personality
your
eye
to see
memory
to keep
itself

in memory
like a flock
of butterflies
glow worms
fireworks
through
bonfires
on
midsummer
night
your
night
Jaan
John

suddenly you discover that your world and your self have no
centre you have no place which you can stand and call home these
souls your own lost soul but what does this HOME mean everything
is let loose and awakes into life stones into seagulls sand into
sandpipers

and suddenly you see that nothing even yourself is either inside
or outside but on the border in the present time in wind that

being itself is but a border where the sparks of life thought and words light for an instant like moths which have flown into fire and then ash falls down from the blade of fire always on the side where WAS is written and from the other side come new butterflies new lives new loves and they too catch fire like moths which have flown into lamplight which means they are caught by fire burnt into ash this is beautiful and terrible the only question is who can see it is it a similar spark a speck of spacedust leaving a fiery trace seen on the backdrop of a constellation

and this question grows bigger grows into an eclipse covering the moon covering the stars covering meaning so that finally over your head there is only a huge black eye reflecting this awkward half-articulate question your doubt in the world and in yourself a spider's thread coming carried by wind from somewhere on the other side which goes through all that you believed is firm and real but has not been for a long long time

this huge black eye of another heaven full of questions full of doubt full of the same endless thirst that no philosophy no literature no art can quench it is the thirst of the world itself of all the cells roots mouths and intestines for fire thirst of life for life this thirst and yet something else something is wrong something is false the centre is not in the centre the circle is not round a cause cannot have an effect Achilles cannot reach the turtle the arrow stands in every instant at a different place and all Cretans are liars they say it themselves as I too

believe no sentences including this one do not believe Jaan Kaplinski himself and his poems he hasn't believed himself for many years now but he doesn't know what this really means this him this self and this believing two points and a line but if neither of the points is at a certain place where is the line where am I where is self where is everything where is nothing

you my
forgotten
self
you my
lost
meaning

is the blood
a better
companion
on passage
through
vessels
through
the heart

do you
hear
my
silence
do I
hear
your
voice

something
throbbing
coming
going

white
horse
black
horse
again
and again

new stones
pebbles
under
the wheels

new sparks
in the dark
between
two days
two white
pages

is it snow
that
covers
all the words written
on stones
in
books

birth
death
data

rest in peace
I am
the resurrection
and the life

in my Father's house
are many
mansions

rest in peace
personal
pro–

noun
on a
granite
plaque

why have I
carried you
with me
always
selfstone
stone
self

fingers
get tired
feet
stumble
on
hummocks
between
hummocks
in marshy
water
or on
those other
stones

mossy
round
stones
with
no
words
no
inscriptions
no

meaning
stones
amidst
foam
flow
flux
murmur
rising
from
your tired
legs
into ears
head

reminder
of rising
blood
pressure
of memory
memorial
stones
that
crushed
you fingers
that once
wanted
to become
young
and happy
become
five
ten
childish
fingers
in
running

219

water
and wind

memory
what do you
keep
in memory
from
your beginning
what was
before
what
will be
after
you

what remains
to me
only
the knowledge
that some
have to
carry
little Jesus
to the other
shore
some
death
some the
same memory
heavy
growing
stone

some
them-
selves

and there
is no
difference
between
this Jesus
this me
this death
and stone

in the
midst of this
life
only
one death
and whether
you are
you
or me
there
is always
something
bringing
every vision
back
into
the same
memory
and
pain

and whether you are you or me there is always something
bringing every vision back into the same memory and pain

earth watches
in the same way
over
every
flying
stone and
bird

life-giver life-taker earth the anchor-stone the gravestone of us all
big old lonely stone in the dark emptiness – who are you – I
would like to ask something from you I don't know yet what it
should be but soon it will be too late

something
glowing
red
in white
something

living
flame
heart
in us
in snow
everything
that
goes out
is extinguished
expires

cave
a grave candle
has melted
into
snow

the
world is
just ash
a resting
place
for dead
flames
a
glow
a dying
out
in the
middle
deep
below
everything
that
has
ever been
has been
fire
and

we
come
back
as
ash
as stones
as sparks
some
fall
back
meet
again
fall
apart

fall
into
memory
through
memory
where there
is no
difference
between
falling
particles
of dust
ash
or stars
through the
huge
empty
emptiness

a dying
man

in every
child
in every
dying
man
an
unborn
child

in every
thought
another
thought
other fingers
rummaging
through
someone's
fingerbones
a saw
sawing
itself
in half

mewling
of a
child
traces
of wind
on stone
poems
books
you can
call
your
own

do you
still
come
back
whatever
you have
or haven't
been

but
despite
you
without
you
me is
something
even worse

time

something
salty
coarse
anchor chain
sinking
through
you
never
reaching
the
ground
and poetry
fingerless
hand
rummaging
through

itself
through
white sea-
sand
songs and
destiny
without
finding
the sword
only
soldiers'
fingerbones
our fingerbones
strangers' ones
without
finding
the sword
only
sword wounds

new ones
old ones

but
still
there is
something
else
something
sharp
glittering
somewhere
on
a reef
through
sand and

water

far
far
from
everything
something
else

a single
piercing
pin
a
dot
without
an i

in this
merciless
confused
continuity

stone
beside
a stone
and
between
them
always
yet
another
stone

where
is there
a place

a slit
for a
knife
for
an
understanding

and
whence
all this
light

whence
language
words

a hole
in
a hole
a dot
without
an i

in the
going
away
into
the blue
far
away

far away
a sword
there
under
many

waters
under
many
seas

a skylark

beam
of light
tiny
shadow
like
a sword-
blow

through us
every
moment
what
it is
time
dripping
through
a desert
or sea-
sand
shadows
setting
into
the
ocean

where
are
you from

oblivion
where are
all these
borders
things
from

long bench
fire
breadknife

tick
tock

or
are you
the same
drop
of oblivion
grown
around
a speck
of stardust
a crystal
of
ice

becoming
a hieroglyph
a feather
in the
earth carpet
thaw water
down
downstream
past

everything
else

drop of
memory
clay
for
making
an
Omar Khayyam
a mug
a crocus

memory
oblivion
remembering
forgetting

black
white

raven
snow
owl

who are
nearly
the same
and
still
between
them
the whole
world

on

which side
of the wall
your
eyes
your mouth

that see
speak
eat
for you
writer

what
do you
pay
them all
these
feet
carrying
you
the stomach
digesting
your
food
for you

how
much
easier
have they
made
your life

how
do you
pay

them
your
self
who
exists
instead
of you
is your-
self
instead
of you

a net
holding
together
potatoes
hands
conscience
intestines
feet
or are you
something
even worse

a parasite
a tapeworm
a self
inside
your
self
inside
this
instant
this body
this
now

living
loathsome
wriggling
bundle of
shadows
that
doesn't
allow
the eyes
to see
mind
to
remind
itself
life
to live
eyes
fingers
understanding
reaching
deeper
inside
this
instant

tape-
worm
of memory
that
doesn't
allow you
to dissipate
to forget
to be

how is

it possible
to be
anything
but
free

as if
you
couldn't
exist
without
this
tapeworm
that wants
to get
its
share of
everything
to tie
together
all the
poems
moments
pain
with a fine
red
ribbon
for you
who are
wrapped
into a
pretty
ornamented
sheet
of paper
a wet

mossy
stone
from
the stream
of memory
consciousness
grown
around
a random
particle
of
ancient
ash

maybe
carrying
traces
of lips
of poems
that
have been
have left
vanished
gone

traces
left
into sand-
stone
lime
-stone
petrified
sea-
bed
sea-
weed

forest

from their

waves

from their

flowing

stones

I have

just been

put

together

this flow

still

in my

blood

my ears

how easy it is to look for to find a metaphor or whatever it should
be called and to let it live its own life in the hands of a poet
everything then begins to move everything gets wings and
becomes light on the other side under the earth the rivers flow
from the sea back to the mountains and there in the mouth of an
underworld river is a white rock that is as light as everything else
and this stone takes flight and sings it sings for you all the songs
you wanted to sing it rises the rock rises like a skylark and flies
for you everywhere you wanted to fly where then of course to the
southern seas no not to the palm trees and pretty girls further to
the south where some islands are lost in the silence of the Pacific
Falkland Macquarie Kerguelen Bouvet somewhere somewhere in
the world there must be something that is unstained and new but
all this is only poetry nobody believes it but why couldn't it be
true from generation to generation from age to age everything has
become heavier and heavier things people rocks notes and sounds
only words have become weightless and I too cannot put them
back bring them back to their meanings but still this weight is not
in us is not in the things this is the weight of borders it is a
weight that is between us that separates us from everything the
weight of names of memory of continuity of regularity the weight
of this everyday thing that has been called life the weight of dust
from the streets that has been ground from everything from words
rocks silence ourselves something that is like a grey flour but
really isn't grey flour that maybe somewhere is called truth and
reality but I cannot I cannot even for who knows when who
knows when again

I fall
back
there
like
a tapeworm
a parasite
into
my own
intestines

and still
there
is nothing
inside
that has
not
been
outside

for an
instant
you
are there
built
of rays
and
echoes
of
the
universe

shadow
not person
mirror
not self

somebody's
glance
which has
looked
an instant
into
you

what islands
then
what
whales
what clouds
swimming
back
into you
what a
sea
Thalassa
Thalatta
at your
orchard
gate
what a sea
what a sea
what a sea

what
a
return
of
the soul
return
of all
killed
skylarks

bards
kings

their
return
home

to
Revala
Sakala

to the Antipodes

Falkland
Bouvet
Kerguelen

coming
back
turning
back
returning
this way
a way
away

new
flaming
as fire
coming
back
to the
beginning

beginning

anew
as fire
as flames

fiery to die in flames
fiery to be born in flames
flames my friends my own kin

returning
being
reborn
in flames
come
come
back
away
your
own
way

but
don't
forget
who
what
I
have been
here
for
ten
eleven
years
lying
on
my
face

on
the earth

where
my
chiefs
my
kings
have died
have been dead
seven
eight
thousand
years

is there
a
place
for any-
thing
between
us
between
me
and them
me
and their
coming
back

for any-
thing
thing
but
fire
but
sleep

lying
on
my
face
in a
dry
river
bed

until
they
believe
pain is pain
sighs are sighs
tears are tears

until

the bed
boards
are
wholly
rotten

mugworts
rise
through
me
through
the bed
boards

until
they
believe
in the

death
sleep

I
am
sleeping

with Osmi
who was sick

for
seven years
eight summers

together
with rocks
words
countries

with Lembity from leole rebel chief who had his head cut off sent
to Rome with four kings electedby the Estonians and sent to
negotiate with the Knights and put to death by them hewn into
pieces

in Paide Pala Muhu Tartu Tallinn Estonia Livonia Alesia
Wounded Knee

sleep
filling
fields
waste lands
wheels
and
chimneys
up
to the
brim

what then
remains
for
the awakening
what stays
awake

if even
sleep
is full
of the same
dust
and grinding
of
teeth

something
deeper
yet
behind
this sleep
this dream
this
waking

on the
other
side
in a
huge
huge
sea

islands

Kerguelen

an
other
dream
full ot
southbound
swans and
sails

your flight
your wings
wings
above
these
islands
seas

islands
islands
archipelagoes

full of
your
mute
feathers

flakes
of snow
covering
everything

snow
always
coming
back
ice
glaciers
coming
coming

do you
hear me
soul
my little
soul

do you hear

is
every
body
tired
asleep
is fire
still
awake

is fire
the
lost
soul
self

tired of a sigh
coming who believes
back tears
until
ash of the bed
burnt is rotten
feathers the fire
burnt is off
songs
white even
flakes if you
covering
everything do
all
Ugandi not
Uganda
Valgatabalve come
Kalahari
Kerguelen I
still
the king is dead refuse
the kings are dead to say
the gods are dead welcome
glaciers are coming yes
hello
covering everything to
it
we live in the ice age to
ice
still
my dream if it
a dream only comes
fire my own kin it
comes
who believes by
a song itself

un–
wanted
un–
greeted

ice
death
weariness

everything
except
the
lost
soul

o

knots
tighten

I
am
falling
back

but
where

no
direction
no
centre

only
your

pride
about
having
looked
into
the eyes
of
the glacier
having told it
something
to
its
face

ah
let
it all
be
let me
my-self
stay
with
its
pride
in the
white
glittering
ice
of death
sleep

there
is

is

only
this flame
fire
far
away
high
up
on
the
hill

grave candle
tallow lamp
from
the
Palaeolithic

fire
flame

at
least

for the
sake of
this
splendid
dream
where I
could
stay
with your
non-existent
heather
forests

three kings
four kings
Melchior
Kaspar
Balthasar
Lembitu of Leole

Crazy Horse
Dull Knife

37 degrees South
58 degrees North

Macquarie
Sakala
Muhu
Kerguelen

we live in the ice age
we live in the ice
we live
we

still
who you
were
when
you came
you
are
no
more

when you
go
away

come
back

one
single
spark
remained
of
all those
words

weariness
red
yellow
poppies
looking
down at
you
from
high up
come
nearer
come
to
mind

come
back
from
oblivion

some-
where
in some-
body
it
lives

comes
back
to
life
again

fire
flame

soul

and

LAULA LAULA PAPPI
SING SING PRIEST

MAGA MAGAMAS
SLEEP A SLEEP
SLEEP
ASLEEP
SLEEP

POEMS WRITTEN
IN ENGLISH

I remember it well:
it is one of these engravings. Perhaps
an Albrecht Dürer or Moritz Schwind
from a book I have looked for a hundred times
when I was sick and alone in our Tartu flat
with my temperature rising. The heavy book
was on my lap. I entered it
somewhere in the middle. I was close to a German town
at the riverside. The water was still, there was no wind:
the great glassy medieval silence filled me
with a strange feeling. There was no movement,
no time, no life. Or perhaps movement,
time and life were too slow for me to perceive,
as I wandered there under the voiceless walls,
windows and trees – no leaf trembled. A man,
barefooted, was sitting on the hill and reading a book.
I passed by, I went through many cities,
hills and landscapes. I arrived in the 20th century
where everything is moving so fast, where everybody
is so nervous, where the medieval stillness
is broken to pieces, shattered, become a whirl
of colours, lines, spots, sounds and shrieks.

I came out of the book at a picture by Edvard Munch,
full of the same fear and anguish as in the days
of my childhood, days and nights of fever.
It was long ago. I had nearly forgotten the book.

Now, forty years later I recalled what had happened.
I found the book. I found the engraving, a Dürer.
It was very much the same. Only when I put on my glasses
did I discover some very minute changes. Some leaves,
some hairs in St Anthony's beard had moved.
He had bowed his head an inch lower than before.

I would like to know if he had turned the page of his book,
but I didn't see the letters through the haze
that was rising from the river or from my own eyes.

*

Fatherland
homeland
words become meaningless
in the Western world
in modern poetry

Words losing their
(eco)logical niche as fish
as suffocating fish from some
used up lake
some waterless body of water

I am a fish too
a fish from a lake called
Estonia
perhaps you know where
it is – somewhere
not far from Thule
on the other side of
the Iron Curtain
somewhere in the colourless
voiceless void
far far from everything
civilised
Homeland
where our spirits
have been living for two
thousand years
on the same place
in the same tree

Could I have thought they
would drive them out
would chop me down

chop down my old
sacred home-tree
dry up my sacred home-lake
my roots, my old roots
lie naked in the
voiceless void left
of my homeland
home-wood
home-lake

I have little voice
little voice left
to talk in Polish
or in any
other foreign language
used up dried up
suffocating
in the bottom
of some foreign lake
some foreign city
they call Warszawa or Kraków
somewhere
beyond the edge of the world
full of elegant
multicoloured fish
poets artists
souvenir shop jewellers
and good Catholics
whom I never really met

They asked me
do I feel myself
at least a bit Polish
what could I answer them
what did I answer them
an Estonian non-Catholic

non-Protestant
a fish from a far-off lake
looking upon them
through these multicoloured
reefs and waves
what words have they
heard from my mouth
grown up in another language
in another world

Yes I think I talked with Tadeusz Różewicz
in a dream in a coffee-house
at the sea bottom
where there was a Mickiewicz
and many doves white gray and blue
he drank beer and probably
asked me about something
but I am sure he didn't hear
what I was trying to answer
through the salty sparkling water
I a fish from Estonia

Of course I am not mute nor dumb
fishes have their speech
their languages
but to listen to them you must
have very expensive microphones and
tape recorders
and much patience
and it may take a long time to wait
for a fish to come out of water
and speak
Indo-European
to foreign writers and correspondents

His father was Polish indeed
dead in Russia long long ago
and his brothers and sisters have
become fish in an unknown sea
and are dead or gone or lost
In a midday dream I swam over the
sunlit warm bottom of the sea of Kraków
there were many nice colourful fish
with sparkling scales and voices
I tried to speak to them
It made no sense
they had beautiful voices
as they talked Indo-European
swimming over multicoloured corals

Then I awoke here
in a dried up ancient salt lake
called Tallinn
with some foreign books and papers in my hand
'est-ce qu'il fait très froid
en Pologne... en Estonie?'
asked Wisława Szymborska
or someone else

Light comes in through windows
cyclones come across Scandinavia
fish we buy and cook are caught somewhere
very far from here in the Antarctic seas.

*

I feel sorry for you white paper.
I feel sorry for you white snow.
I feel sorry for you white clouds.
I feel sorry for you white sky.
I feel sorry for you white earth.
I feel sorry for you white people.
I feel sorry for you white birds.
I feel sorry for you white fish.
I feel sorry for you white grass.
I feel sorry for you white colour
a relic, a memory of a past pure world
we have taken from the children of our children
and thrown away.

*

A lullaby that never ends,
your lullaby red sandstone,
your lullaby river,
your lullaby distant highway
your lullaby Good Night.

*

After many bitterly cold days
in mid-January I stood at the window,
and then, suddenly, I saw them again:
light bluish shadows on fresh-fallen snow,
shadows of young pine-trees, of children's castles,
of a broken ski of a lost mitten,
and shadows of snow itself, myriads
of living and playing shadows, everything
suddenly alive, full of colour and meaning,
and of reminders that I should be
not here but somewhere else,
perhaps in my country home where shadows are more blue
and snow more white with tiny strips of stray birch bark,
trembling in gusts of wind which comes
from far away over open fields and barren groves,
and brings to my ears the faint sound of rolling crumbs of snow
and some distant calls of chickadees.

*

God is smile. When I met him
for the last time I didn't understand it
although I knew something
about the blue flower. Buddha
showed Kasyapa and Kasyapa's smile.
God is but a Buddha's smile, Buddha's
not taking seriously not forgetting
us lost children in a lost world.
Blue flower, *blaue Blume*.
I was twenty-two sitting on a wood block
in melting snow. The sun was shining.
It was March. Then it happened.

It lasted for two days. I understood
everything I had the time to think of.
There were no barriers, no stops, no thoughts,
only a clear flow of understanding, of knowing
everything and beyond and through that
His blue clear smile
penetrating everywhere, present everywhere
so fully, so absolutely that I do not know
where his smile ended and he himself began
or if there was any difference at all
between the smile and the one who smiles
and the blue flower that is dropping
one after one, year after year,
its petals that vanish
in the sky that is as blue and has
the same pure odour of springwind and melting snow.

*

Something stirring,
some deep pain waking up
in the left side of my breast.
I know, I know well,
I have overcome, transcended
the repressive monotheism
and naïve ethnocentricity.
I have learned from you as everybody else.
But why then this something,
this movement, this urge when I hear
your voice Israel calling home
your lost sheep, your lost genes,
your lost ashes
from all the four winds of the world?
A pain, an urge, a something
rising from the left side of my breast,
becoming a poem, an answer.

O yes, O yes
Rabbi Baal Shem Tobh.
O yes
Rabbi Nachman of Braclaw.

O yes
Rabbi Martin Buber of Vienna.
We all are lost in the matter, lost in the darkness, lost
in the world, in ourselves, in our thoughts and dreams,
lost even in our longing for the lost home, lost in the
call that calls us, lost in the names of things and
persons, lost in the name of God himself, lost in the tears
wept for your sake Jerusalem.

*

Karl Barth, Paul Tillich, Karl Rahner.
Some more immortals with two-thousand-year-old peaches
and volumes of collected works
somewhere on the Western Mountains.
Theology never dies. Blue smoke thickens
into new ghosts, letters, books, commentaries,
snails, seaweed, sponges. Hour by hour
thickens the half-living crust
on the oaken board-planks
and the cheeks of the sails get wrinkled and sooty,
longing for open seas and fresh winds,
smells and colours of foreign lands:
cedar of Lebanon, balm of Gilead,
silk of China and girls of the South, singing
in strange tongues and looking strangely
without fear and shame into your eyes, through your eyes,
through ourselves. Foreign girls
with light steps and tiny silver bells
on their hips and sleeves.
But if I had no love I would be a

kymbalon alalazon
alalazon
alala
lala
la

   *

Coming home.
Three kilometres along the bank of the frozen river.
Only some open spots left.
Dozens of ducks quacking, swimming, splashing,
diving their heads into the icy water
and shaking them.
Some people standing on the bridge,
throwing them crumbs of bread.
Some lanterns in the dusk
and snow falling falling
silently, softly, and in this silence
suddenly a voice calling us,
reminding us there is something that is
more even than life. Silence. Beauty.
Falling snow. Perfect crystals. Flakes.
Harmony. Beauty. *To kalon.*
Snowflakes become drops of water
on my face. In my beard.
Sound of water buried, shut
in the silence of snow. Voice
of God. More even than God.
Snowflakes. Voice of Water. *Mizu no oto.*
Vox aquae. Vox Dei.

*

Om svabhavasuddah sarva dharmah. No selfhood.
Everything without own-being, without selfhood.
No self. No own. No hood.
No ness. No ism. No tion. No thing.
All melting away, water trickling
from the roof, from the icicles.
Water drip-dropping. Winter's heart broken.
Winter's eyes wet. Some mountains
are mountains again. Some rivers are rivers again.
Some universals are real. Universalia sunt realia.
Some are not. Realia non sunt realia.
Icicles melting. Water dripping. You can
take one of them and put it in your mouth.
No smell. No taste. No colour. Pure ice
melting into pure water.
One into another. One into itself.
No self. No own. No ness. No thing.
One in one. One in all. All in one.
Spring sky in a falling drop.
Li Po in a Seteria grain. Universe in a grain of sand.
All in all. River river again.
No self. Water again water. Drip. Drop.

*

Wild geese flying overhead
from NE to SW,
flock after flock.
Yellow and red leaves
falling
on already fallen leaves
with a strange sound.

It is so still. No wind.
Smoke rising vertically.
Silence. Suddenly I hear it:
there are
no more grasshoppers left.
They have died,
killed by night frosts
or endless rain that has changed
our roads into muddy strips of earth.
And I do not know if I would have liked
to go South with you wild geese
or fall silent with you
summer grasshoppers,
lying dead in the withered grass.

*